# INSTAGRAM MARKETING

The Ultimate Guide to Grow Your
Instagram Account, Build Your
Personal Brand and Get More Clients

*By*

**David James Miles**

# TABLE OF CONTENTS

# DESCRIPTION

Instagram is extremely unique in so many ways and is the combination of almost all the social media sites available and then some. Photos, videos, music, color, trends, tags, stories and messages: it's all there. It has the potential to support many brands and business types around the world. The continued growth does not show any indication that it will end any time soon. It's time for you to join in the fun and get your slice of the pie. With 1 billion users, it's big world to take advantage of!

Use the tools, visit the websites and apps, and explore the world of Instagram for yourself. All of these guidelines will help you build an impactful brand or your small business on Instagram. Build profit, fuel growth and create a better, more recognizable, successful brand, starting today!

# INTRODUCTION

Presently you will enter the universe of Instagram! How phenomenal would it be to get your things and brand seen by more people, grow a strong number of customers who really relate to your picture, and get paid? Instagram is your most logical option on the off chance that you truly need to make six figures with your business.

Since Instagram has in excess of 750 multi month to month individuals (This beats Twitter!), various brands are finding ways to deal with participate with the Instagram site and increase with contributed customers who hold returning for extra ventures.

However, it's not just the numbers you should consider. It's the overall public using Instagram.

Instagrammers are purchasers. Various investigations have appear over the most recent five years alone that Instagram's system has developed in buying power by clients, and it will just develop more.

When you set up pictures and pictures in Instagram and have a decent eye for what clients like, you can pitch deals to them with no hard exertion on your part. You make an intrigue dissimilar to no other; they generally state words usually can't do a picture justice, so make the most of your pictures.

Clients head to Instagram and other online life locales for various reasons, what we need to concentrate on is buying power. So the exercise of the story is this: Instagram helps convert uninvolved clients into beyond any doubt customers.

In the event that you're new to the Instagram world, no burdens. All that you need to know to exhibit your picture on Instagram is verified here. Additionally, in case you aren't a fledgling, I have all that you have to know directly here in this part, too, take a gander at it as a boost with some new tips for you.

# CHAPTER 1

# IS INSTAGRAM RIGHT FOR YOU?

We have already established the fact that Instagram is a very popular platform, and you might be missing a lot of opportunities if you are not in it yet. But like any other business decision, you should consider everything before you jump in.

Is Instagram the right channel for your online marketing? If so, what are the best strategies to market your brand on Instagram?

Sure. There are around 106 million Americans using the platform, which is a massive potential audience for you to grow, but there are pointers to consider to figure out if this channel is really suitable for your business.

## What are the Age Demographics of Your Target Audience?

The main factor to consider is the fact that majority of Instagrammers are between 18 and 35 years old. Is this the ideal age range for your target audience? It makes sense for a fashion brand or a food chain to invest its resources to market on Instagram, but what if you're catering to the needs of retirees? Or what if your business mainly serves other businesses in your industry (B2B) such as IT solutions, accounting, or tax compliance?

If your target audience is not really within the age demographics of Instagrammers, this channel may not be on top of your priority platforms. This is a reality that you must carefully consider before you even sign up for an Instagram business account.

But if you have a retail brand that directly sells products to customers (B2C) or if your services primarily appeal to the younger audience, then it makes sense to build a massive presence on Instagram.

## Can B2B Companies Use Instagram?

Yes, businesses that are offering products and services to other businesses can still use Instagram. The same goes for businesses that are not mainly catering to the needs of younger demographics. The key is to develop a content strategy that will effectively showcase your business or brand.

Remember, boosting sales is not the only benefit that Instagram can provide for your business. With the right strategy, you can use Instagram to share your company culture, allow exclusive access to behind-the-scene events, create an engaging platform for your employees, and many more.

### Is Your Target Audience Mobile?

You also need to understand that Instagram is a mobile app. Hence, your audience can only see and engage with your brand if they are on mobile. Usually, those on Instagram are on the go, and they tend to be younger than facebook users who often check their accounts using desktop computers.

### Does Your Audience Want Your Brand on Instagram?

If your target audience is on Instagram, the next factor to consider is the possibility that they want to see your brand on the platform. Based on a research conducted by GrowEpic, the top brands on Instagram are related to retail, food, beauty, and health.

However, your success on this platform is not strictly limited to your brand. Engaging content is still key. For example, NASA is far away from these industries, but they have around 14.1 million followers and one post can garner an average of 400,000 likes. You just need to really know your audience and share photos and videos that they want to see in their Instagram news feeds.

### Do You Have the Skills and Resources to Effectively Use Instagram as a Marketing Platform?

Instagram is a powerful tool that will allow you to engage with your customers if you do it right. But before you can reap the rewards of customer engagement, you need to work hard on it. Again, engaging content is key in effective Instagram marketing so you must have the resources and skills to produce photos and videos that will stir the interest of your target audience.

Remember, Instagram is predominantly a photo-sharing social media channel, so your content should be designed to fit this model. Hence, you might need to redesign your content from the ground up and make sure that your brand can still convey the right message without using too much text. Do you have the skills to comply with this requirement? If not, you may need to hire an Instagram marketer or outsource the job to an online marketing agency.

Aside from the quality of content, you should also consider quantity. You must regularly post content that asks for comments from your followers. On average, you should aim share 1-2 posts every day. Don't go beyond this limit as your followers may unfollow you for posting too often, especially if your posts are all about products.

## Instagram Should Not Be Your Only Channel for Online Marketing

While Instagram can provide amazing benefits for your online marketing efforts, it should only be part of a greater marketing mix.

For example, you should not expect a big surge of online traffic from Instagram because the platform is not designed for that. Instagram engagement is more about likes and comments and not clickthroughs mainly because you can't include links to your posts. You can only direct your followers to your website on your account biography.

If you want to increase clickthroughs, you should definitely include other online marketing strategies such as Search Engine Optimization and Facebook Marketing.

Also remember that just like Facebook, Instagram is also a "Pay-to-Play" platform. This is in fact among the biggest misconceptions businesses often have. Some marketers who are not familiar with the platform think that all of their followers will see their posts. Instagram's algorithm puts a limit on the number of followers who can see your content. If you want your posts to reach everyone, you have to pay for the privilege. Without boosting your post as an advertisement, only a small percentage of your followers may engage in your content.

Hence, in considering Instagram as a marketing channel for your brand, you should also consider the amount you're willing to invest in this platform.

In summary, you should consider the following factors to determine if Instagram is right for your business:

- Age Demographics of your target audience (Instagrammers are between 18 and 35 years old)

- Your target audience's device preference (Instagram is a mobile app)

- The nature or industry of your brand (Successful brands on Instagram are mainly related to food, drinks, health, beauty, retail, and lifestyle)

- Your skills and resources to regularly produce engaging content

- Your marketing mix and overall online marketing strategy

Once you have determined that your brand can take advantage of Instagram, the next step is to define your target audience and make sure that your brand is properly aligned with your customers and not the other way around.

# CHAPTER 2

# BASIC FEATURES

The characteristics of Instagram as a social platform whose contents are in relation to visuals. Its premises on sharing and viewing graphics, videos, and photos. Its operations and plugins are categorized on its contents: visuals. The idea that it is used only by young people is very wrong. In this section, you will be guided systematically into the features of Instagram for either beginners or professionals. By beginners, it means people that are new to Instagram while professionals mean those familiar or even have an account on the platform. Some of the basic features with their operations include:

## The filter options

While uploading pictures on Instagram, the filter is the section which enables you to add enhancements on the photos to be uploaded. These filters make the pictures to look like studio edited ones. They are galvanized with features such as vintage, contrast, light, grayscale, soft glow, and lots more. Try uploading pictures and use this filter to create a special effect on them. Many influencers of Instagram claim that using these filters can make you outstanding among users of Instagram because the sense of filtration is typical only to you. Try it and grow your profile.

## Like Button

One of the commonest features on Instagram is the like button. This platform can barely operate without features such as this. This is like an authorization given to fellow users to comment, follow or do anything to your post on the platform. The like button enables users to give either pleasing or unpleasing undertone remark on your posts. With the like button, lots of transformation like increment in the number of followers and the benefits that follow is activated.

The like button works in two places: it can be used on the home page, and it can be used as a user's dashboard. When the like button is used at the general page, it only gives remarks on the posts while when it is on the user's dashboard, the person becomes a 'follower.'

### The Iconosquare feature

This is a form of a hashtag that is typically used to track campaigns. The performance report of the campaigns is what Iconosquare brings to you. You will be able to see relating data of the hashtag and even the growth alongside engagement of it on the campaign you have created.

### The @ feature on Instagram

This is used basically for direct comment. This is for comment on posts on the platform. One could comment by tapping on the comment bubble through the person's username or type @ alongside the username.

### The Word Suggestion content

This feature has been designed to help while typing on the platform. With a few words, you will be given any suggestion to make it easier for you to type. In the cases of comment, you will see related words while searching for a username. You will have related usernames.

### Instagram set up operations

To download the Instagram app, one needs to consider the iOS of the medium to download it. If you have Android, you will download from 'Google Play.' If you have an iPhone, you will download from the 'App store.' Search these stores, you will, with ease, locate the app.

### Registering your Instagram Account

After downloading the Instagram app, you will need to open an account. The app should create a 'shortcut icon' on your homepage after installation: if it didn't check your installed apps. Register your account or log in if you have an account already.

## Creating your Instagram Account

Upon the location and clicking on the app, you will need to create a username and password. Your username can be any name combination. At this point your creativity is needed, the username can be a nickname. Care must be taken to use a name familiar to the people in order to facilitate the location and gaining of followers quickly. For example, you might consider using a clip of your first name and surname in uppercase or lowercase as 'TIMSAM' or 'timsam' for Timothy Samuel. After the username, use a password that is familiar with other platforms. You will surely need to add your email account which you could create one for the account. You can choose to add your phone number or not.

## Uploading your profile photo

After you have created your account, as part of the process of perfect and strong Instagram account, you will need to add your profile picture. The picture can be taken immediately as you open your account but uploading an existing picture with high quality is highly recommended. Select 'Done' when you have uploaded the picture.

## Friends and Family found on Instagram

For capitalization of your account to the full fledge, you will need to follow people that will share your pictures, and you do same to theirs. You can consider giving them your username or search from your account. With increment in followers, there are lots of benefits attached to it.

## Adding and Following on Instagram

To be added to an account, you will be on the followers' list. You can follow and be followed respectively. Addition of a user will as well enable you to follow too. However, to randomly add people, you could click on the 'cog icon' on the home screen and click on 'invite friends.' With this, contacts of people around your vicinity will be suggested.

## Connect to Social Media

You have an option on the app to search your phonebook directly. Simply click on 'My Contact,' and you will be prompted to search. Contacts with the Instagram account will come up, click on 'Follow' to add them to your account. Then, click on the home icon to return to the home of your account which should show the added accounts.

## Home Screen

The icon looks like a house. It will automatically refresh itself when your photo has like, comment or when one of your friends add photos. The home will be updated with data, however.

## Profile

The brief story created about you is your profile. The file card at the corner of the home screen contains your profile. Other things at this corner are photos, "following" and "Followers."

## Privacy on Instagram

On the 'Edit my Profile' button, you can restrict the people that can view your profile. This is not encouraging, however, for a business person.

## Privacy Off/on

When your privacy is turned off, anybody, even outside Instagram, can view your account. When it is switched on, only people following you can view your account.

## News Feed

Photos, graphics, and videos are what is contained in the news feed.

You can refresh the page by simply swiping it down. The news feeds are selected randomly; you scroll up or down.

## Viewing comments from your Friends and family

The photo at the top left of your home screen is used to view people that have commented on your photo. Before clicking on it, there is something in grey color. It is meant to give you information about the comment.

## Adding comment

Simply tap the speech bubble at the home screen which will prompt a new page to enable you to write your comment. Send it, and your name will appear right under the comment.

## Attached Links

This feature enables people to be prompted to either another user's account or website. It is strategically attached to the account to enhance it. Most likely, it is a business account. If you click on surf new page, you can return to your home by tapping the back button on your phone.

## The # Hashtag meaning

This feature is used to publicize a given post. By publicizing it, very many users will have access to the post. When you are using the hashtag, make sure there is no space between it and your post to avoid misunderstanding of your post. Additionally, when a hashtag is added to a post, it appears in blue. There are various reasons Instagram users use the hashtag. Some of these reasons include; promotion of business, gaining more followers, connecting to people that have the same idea and specialization as theirs, etc.

The hashtag enables you to search based on your specific interest on the platform. Your interest varies alongside many other things such as a book, mountain, etc. For instance, you could search with this #mountains. This will give you varying posts relating to your interest. Also, you will see profiles that have the same interest as you. The profiles that will be prompted will be top leading users who will teach you how best to construct your account too.

## iOS, Android or Window icon

This particular icon is used to add photos. You can access it by clicking on the blue icon and then the circle at the bottom of the icon. Your gallery will be accessed automatically, and you can add your photo.

## Followers icon

This is used to show the people that are following you in numbers. By followers, it simply means those people that your posts, whatsoever, will appear in their news feed. When you click on this icon, you will be able to see pictures of these people and either white color (to show you are following them) or blue button (to show you are yet to follow them).

## Star symbols

This is technically referred to as the explore icon. It enables you to access a new page with a square at its top to type your information. With this icon, you can individualize your search. By individualizing, it means that you can search an account by hashtag or nickname. This facilitates a random and quick response from these people when you post. You can as well access their profiles upon searching.

# CHAPTER 3

# THE BENEFITS OF USING INSTAGRAM FOR BUSINESS

The increasing popularity of social media makes it a matter of urgency and utmost importance for your business to be advertised on these platforms if you are really serious about creating a viable funnel for directing traffic to your business and gradually growing it.

If you have chosen to promote your business on Instagram, what do you stand to gain from that decision?

There are some valuable benefits you can derive from driving your business growth with Instagram. Let's have a look at some of the best benefits you can derive from it:

### Increased engagement

While many brands concentrate on using Twitter and Facebook to increase their online engagement with their customers, they oftentimes overlook the potential of Instagram to help increase their engagement. If you have an active Instagram account with valuable content, you have a platform that can increase your engagement levels beyond your imagination.

If you have a new product or service, sharing such information and asking people's opinion about them is a great way to leverage the better engagement to your own benefit. You can equally give your followers a sneak peek into the future of a new project and welcome their input. You may find your followers' input more valuable to the success of the new project.

### You can build trust and personality

One of the easiest ways for brands to generate more engagement is to promote their products with branded content. With Instagram, you can easily leverage the power of your branded content to build a lasting trust amongst your followers. If you can work hard to establish a strong emotional connection with your followers, you will benefit from that feature of Instagram.

If you have a specific brand that you want to promote on the platform, you need to have some amazing ways to promote them to build a good relationship with your audience. One of the methods is by using some behind-the-scene photos. The community usually appreciates employee images if they are professionally shot and are high-quality. Such beautiful images will pass the right information to the community.

The more of such photos you post on your page, the more Instagramers will show interest in your posts. As a result, you can have a good shot at portraying your company in a good light; you increase the company's attractiveness and trustworthiness. That in the long run will impact your business positively as more people become aware of it.

## You can reach your target audience

Instagram may be the perfect place where you can reach your target audience. If your brand is targeting young people, you have an abundance of them on Instagram. A recent study by Jenns Trends shows that almost 4 out of every 10 adults under the age of 30 can be found on Instagram. So, if you are targeting people within that age group, you shouldn't hesitate to create an Instagram account.

 It also attends to the needs of other groups of people as well. A study by Inc.com showed that since 2012, the number of adult Instagram users in the United States has doubled since more adults are getting used to Instagram and a good percentage of the young users are coming of age.

You should try to find out the age group that your brand is targeting and use the right tools, either by Instagram or by a third party, to target your audience. That will boost your chances of reaching your target market on the platform. Regardless of your target audience, you will always find a ready audience on the platform.

## Free advertisement

Advertising, if done right, is crucial to the success of every business. It is one of the most powerful and effective strategies to create awareness to your audience. It has been used for decades for increasing the popularity of a brand. Many companies depend on advertising for their success and have benefited immensely from that decision. That makes it worthwhile to consider the fact that you have access to free advertising.

Instead of contemplating how to raise a small fortune for paid advertisements anywhere, you can enjoy the free advertisement offered by Instagram to increase your reach and gradually build your business, exactly what paid advertisements hope to achieve.

By updating your page regularly with valuable content and attractive photos with the right attributes, your popularity on social media will take a huge leap. In no time, you will reach as many people as you want without spending excessive amounts of money on paid advertising.

This is good news for business owners who are running their businesses on a shoestring budget. Without worrying yourself about how to raise advertising capital, a few minutes are sufficient for you to sign up to an Instagram account and start the race of building huge followers for your account.

**Increased traffic**

This is the major reasons why you have an Instagram account. You want to leverage the services it offers you to build a large portfolio for yourself on the media, all while you drive referral traffic to your website.

Despite the fact that you can directly add clickable links to your posts, it is still a very powerful and result-oriented way to drive an amazing amount traffic to your website. A platform that offers you a higher engagement level than that of Twitter and Facebook has the potential to give you sufficient traffic to keep your business afloat. You only need to do two things: create an impressive bio and do your best to maintain the profile. Don't forget the valuable impact that updating your page with valuable content has. You must leave no stone unturned in your attempt to get your followers addicted to your posts. That will make them pledge their total allegiance to you.

## It offers competitive advantage

If you are an active member of Twitter and Facebook, you will realize that Instagram has less competition compared to those platforms. The implication is that you have a very powerful platform for showcasing your business or brand without the crazy competition you must contend with on both Twitter and Facebook.

The reduced levels of competition on Instagram should be put to good use by capitalizing on the freedom and have less competition so you can expand your reach to as many people as possible.

A recent study by the American Express survey indicated that about 2% of small scale businesses operate on Instagram. That reduces your competition, and you can leverage such reduced competition to create more awareness for your business rather than spend a huge chunk of your time fighting the stiff completion.

## It is ideal for different business sizes

You don't need to entertain unnecessary worry over the size of your business. Instagram is designed to cater to the needs of different companies and brands regardless of the size of their staff.

While some big brands have taken their awareness and popularity to a whole new level, small brands are not left behind. They have mastered the use of the platform to get the most out of it. It is not unusual to see both brands succeeding on the platform by taking advantage of the accommodating nature of the platform.

Some of the big brands that have found success on Instagram include:

- Audi: This auto company is one of the leading names in the auto industry. In recent years, Audi has taken to Instagram to promote its line of cars. The result has been impressive. In just 90 days, two of its photos generated 104,000 and 109,000 interactions respectively. This is an indication that the auto company knows the rules and is applying them correctly. The company used some catchy captions to attract the attention of their followers.

- Starbucks: This is another company that has the know-how of using Instagram to garner engagements. Within a period of two-and-a-half months, the company made 77 posts. With these posts, Starbucks received in excess of 20 million engagements. This is an average of over 270,000 engagements for each of their posts. The most engaging of these posts is the Lemonade post. This post received over 2,000 comments and about 400,000 likes. During that period, the company gained about 1.5 million new followers which translated to a 180% engagement increase.

- Nike: Nike is one of the most popular sportswear manufacturers in the world. Over the course of years, this giant company has used its experience and high-quality images to drive traffic in droves to its Instagram account.

According to a recent study of the biggest brands on Instagram with the highest number of followers, Nike is ranked second, below only to National Geographic.

It is expected that this figure will continue to rise as the company keep playing the game by the rules. With an apt caption, attention-grabbing images, and the other factors, more followers will keep identifying with this sportswear giant.

If you are apprehensive about taking your chances with Instagram, you should consider using Nike's tagline as a piece of advice: Just do it.

Similarly, some small brands have equally benefited from Instagram as I highlighted above. Therefore, the size of your brand is never an excuse for missing out on the plethora of benefits that Instagram offers businesses.

The earlier you commit your business to Instagram, the earlier you benefit from it. Your brand will feel the positive impact of such a wise decision.

# CHAPTER 4

# GROWING YOUR PROFILE AND AUDIENCE

When you first get started on Instagram, you may have a few followers. You may have some people who come from your email list, some followers from your other accounts, and some who just randomly find you when they are searching around the platform. But the truth is, your following in the beginning is going to be pretty small. Many people may not even know you are there. But if you want to extend your reach and get the most out of this platform, then you will need to spend your time learning how to grow your profile and get a larger audience or a larger following.

The good news is there are a lot of different ways that you can grow your audience and therefore your business with the help of Instagram. Let's take some time to look at some of the best secrets and tips that you can follow in order to get more followers to your business page.

## Like and comment on posts in your niche

In one online conference, the CEO of Freshly Picked, Susan Petersen, spent some time talking about how she was able to take her Instagram account and grow it to 400,000 followers at the time (since then she has expanded her following to 800,000). Petersen states that when she was first getting started, she would spend hours each night looking through pictures on Instagram and liking them.

While this may seem like it takes a lot of work, it has worked for many other Instagram marketers in the past. Her advice for businesses and individuals who are trying to grow their reach is to go through and like about five to ten pictures on someone else's account. It is even better if you are able to go through and leave a genuine comment on the account and even follow that person before you leave.

What this does is gets your name out there so that others are able to discover you. First, the owner of the page is going to see that you spent some time on their page and they will want to return the favor. Then the followers of that page will start to see your name pop up and it may pique their curiosity. They may check out your page and even decide to follow you, growing your reach even more from a few minutes of work.

The best way to do this is to find users that are in your niche. You can do this by checking out hashtags that go with your niche or view the followers of some of your favorite names on Instagram. However, make sure that when you do this, you show some genuine personality, rather than being spammy. People can tell when you are trying to use them or spam them, and they will ignore you in two seconds if they feel like that is what you are doing.

## Come up with a theme for the pictures on your page

Write down a few words that you would like people to think about when they come to your page and then use those to help you come up with a theme. This helps to keep the whole page cohesive and looking like it is supposed to go together and can really seem inviting to your followers and any potential followers who are checking out the page.

## Spend your time socializing

The more that you can interact, engage with, and socialize with your followers, the better results that you will get. Make sure that you respond to any comments that are left on your page and spend time commenting and liking posts of other influencers in your industry.

When you are commenting, make sure to put some thought and effort behind the words that you say. Don't just leave a comment like "cute!", because this only takes two seconds and the other person will barely notice it. But don't spend time writing three paragraphs about your own business either, because this will come off as being really spammy. Leave comments that are genuine, ask questions, and encourage others to interact back with you.

## Create your own hashtag and get others to use this too

This is a great way to help out your business because it can ensure that you gain a lot of new content for your own account, and it can build up a community that will really benefit you in the future. The first thing that you need to do here is to create a hashtag that is unique. Double check to see if it is already being used or not. You want to go with something that is unique, easy to remember, and hopefully relates back to your business in some way or another.

Once you have the hashtag created, you can ask your followers to use it. This is going to be successful if you have a specific purpose for the tag. For example, the company known as A Beautiful Mess will encourage their followers to use the hashtag #ABMLifeIsolorful on all of their happy and colorful pictures.

After some of your followers have started to use this hashtag (and make sure that you are using it as well), you can then repost these images from the followers. Make sure that you give the follower credit for the picture, but this provides you with a lot of fresh content that you don't even have to think up. Not only is this method able to build up some community in your industry because you show your followers that you really appreciate their pictures, but it ensures that you get fresh content for your own account.

## Try out a contest

Another thing that you may want to try out is running a contest. If you have a product that you can give away or something that you are willing to give away to help grow your business, then it may be a good idea for you to run a contest. There has to be a catch though. For example, for someone to have a chance of winning the contest, users need to repost a specific image and then tag you in the caption. Or you can invite your followers to use a special hashtag that you design and then use it on their own images.

If you feel like really expanding this out and getting other Instagram names on board, you can consider doing a giveaway. You can get on board with a few other profiles and influencers, and then everyone can be a part of this. This helps to give each profile or business a chance to reach new customers and can be a great way to build up your business like never before.

**Don't forget those Instagram stories**

We already spent some time talking about Instagram stories and all the cool things that you can do with them. But make sure that you actually take the time to use a few of these. You don't necessarily need to do one of these each day, but doing one each week or every few days, can really help you connect with your customers and your followers.

These short clips may not seem like much, but since most of your followers are going to be visual, they can make a big difference. Plus, these videos are more interactive and engaging than traditional posts, so they can help you there as well. Having a good mixture of good posts and stories can help that customer base grow faster than ever before.

**Encourage your followers to take some actions**

It may seem pretty simple, but you will find that your followers are more likely to do something if you actually ask them to do it, rather than just assuming they are going to do it for you. Are you sharing a quote with your followers? Then ask them to like the post if they happen to agree with it. Are you sharing something that is considered relatable or funny? Then ask your followers to tag some of their friends or share the post. Ask your followers some open-ended questions, have them share information about a contest, and find other ways to get the customer engaged as much as possible.

The reason that you do this is to promote some more engagement with the stories that you are doing. The more engagement you get, the higher your account will show up, and the easier it is for new and interested followers to find you. Always ask your followers to show some interest in your posts and you will be amazed at how much more they are willing to participate.

## Add a geotag to your pictures

Another tip that you will want to try out is adding a geotag on your picture. There are a lot of different ways that you are able to do this and you are likely to find a lot of success when it comes to this. For example, if you just took a picture of a really cool new restaurant or a city that you traveled to, and then you decide to use that as one of your postings on Instagram, then take the time to geotag it.

When you add a geotag to your account, other people who used that same kind of tagging are able to see that picture as well. When they see that connection, they may be more willing to follow you because they already noticed that you both have something in common. It may seem like such a little thing, but that small connection is often enough to get people to start following your account. It is a simple thing to do and only takes you a few seconds, but you will be surprised at how many followers you can get with this method.

## Learn what your followers actually like

It isn't going to do you any good to work on a bunch of posts if the things you post are turning your customers off. Remember, your customers have complete control over whether they are going to check you out or not. You must make sure that you are posting things that your customer actually likes. This encourages the followers to stay, gets them to share the information with others, and can get your followers to engage better.

To figure out what things your customers like the most, it is time to do some research. Go through all of those posts and pictures that you have on your profile and check out which ones ended up with the most comments and likes. You can also check out which ones had the least comments and like. This helps you to see what seems to click with your audience and then tailor your message and your future posts to that.

**Link Instagram to some of the other social media sites you are on.**

As a business owner, you probably have other social media platforms that you are going to be on. If you are on Facebook, Twitter, or even have a blog, then you may make the assumption that all of your followers are already following you on each of these platforms. But in reality, they are probably only following you on just one of these platforms.

To help increase the number of followers you have, make sure to send out a quick message on the other platforms you are on to let your followers know they can now follow you on Instagram. You may be surprised at how many followers you are able to get this way.

**Approach other users that are popular in your niche and set up a collaboration**

This is an idea that will ask you to think outside the box a little bit. Take some time to research a few of the other profiles in your niche and then talk to them about doing a collaboration. For this, you can ask them to talk you up or ask if you can take over their account as a guest contributor. You will find that doing an Instagram story takeover can be a lot of fun and can even grow your following in the process. In return, you let that influencer do the same on your page.

What this does is introduces both parties to brand new audiences, audiences that they may have never had a chance to meet without this opportunity. Both of you can benefit as followers hear the stories, learn about the other person, and decide to start following you. The more times you are able to do this, the bigger you can grow your audience.

As you get used to working with Instagram, you will find that the most important thing you can do is grow your audience. The more followers you are able to get to your page, the more potential customers you get to work with. Using some of the tips and secrets that we have above, you will be able to get more followers to your account in no time.

## The Logo

You might have probably written and implemented a social media marketing campaign for your brand but don't have a logo design, yet. A logo is quintessential for your brand and it is critical for any marketing strategy. If your brand has a logo, then people will forever associate your business with that logo whenever they see it. A logo is an important part of branding, especially when you want to make the most of social media and market your business online.

A logo is a part of a brand's identity and it helps potential and existing customers recognize your brand. It also gives brand recognition to your target audience. Whenever someone sees your logo online, it is only natural that they will be curious to learn more about your business and what you do.

So, where does your logo come into the picture in terms of social media marketing? A logo might be small, but it is an important component that contributes to the success of a social media campaign.

As a marketer, it is critical that your existing and potential customers see your brand logo daily. You can embed it on your photos, maybe in one corner; you can add it as a watermark on posts on any of your social media platforms or even use it as your Instagram profile picture. In this manner, your customers will form a perception of your brand that will stay with them forever. The logo plays a very important part in your social media marketing campaign in the following ways.

## Promotes Your Business

How can you identify a business without reading anything about it? You can recognize it from its logo. Doesn't a big, bright M remind you of delicious burgers?

People might wonder how a logo may sell a business out in public.

A logo is an important image with the ability of sticking in the minds of the viewers. Usually, a good and well-structured logo design can promote your business by itself.

A logo conveys a lot and also acts as an introduction to others. You don't have to say much once someone sees your business logo. A good logo says a lot about what you stand for and what you offer, without necessarily uttering any words. For instance, you don't need to be told what that simple tick-like logo on your shoes, training gear or your cap means, do you? The logo tells you about the brand, doesn't it?

## Creates an Identity

At times, content isn't sufficient to get the word out there. All the content you post will not make any sense if your brand doesn't have a sense of identity.

A logo helps create an identity for your brand.

In fact, without a logo, you will also end up like a lot of the other startup marketers on the web who create and post a lot of content in the hopes of generating traffic to their website. This approach might produce some results. Nonetheless, your logo will greatly communicate who you are and what your business is all about.

In many instances, a logo tends to attract people so much that they are curious enough to want to know more about your products and services.

## Shows Professionalism

As a marketer, you need to maintain a certain degree of professionalism. You can display professionalism by doing something as simple as including a logo on every Instagram marketing post you make.

It will make your customers feel comfortable while doing business with you. Additionally, if you have a high-quality and interesting logo, it will make your content and your brand stand out among your competition.

With time, you will realize that a logo might be sufficient to get the audience to want to build a relationship with you. If they like your logo, they will like your creativity and the way you communicate.

For instance, people love the logo of Apple and in fact, they don't mind spending huge sums of money to acquire Apple products to flaunt the logo.

## Who and What You Are

When you start to post and share content on Instagram, it is important to place your logo on your content with the URL of your website.

In turn, your followers will start visiting your website often. This is when you can start to reap the benefits of the content you share. Therefore, start to believe in your credibility. Know that when people trust your credibility and expertise, they will want to be involved with you and your brand.

In Instagram marketing, this is the ultimate objective of any marketer.

A logo does provide a lot of benefits, but there are a couple of things that you must keep in mind before you select a specific logo. You need to carry out an extensive research before you create your logo. Typically, the logo must be perfectly in sync with your brand and theme colors. You need to understand that your logo and your brand will ultimately mean the same thing to the customers.

Select an effective logo name: it needs to be unique and memorable. If your logo involves abbreviations/letters, ensure that it easily rolls off everyone's tongue. It needs to be easy to understand and simple to pronounce.

The logo needs to be pleasing to the eye of the viewer. You need to make it simple and easy to identify with.

In case you are not sure whether your logo will be effective and powerful or not, gather information through focus groups. The easiest way to do this is to create a group and invite people whose opinions you value. Take a little while to evaluate their feedback and then you can create a logo.

## Create the Perfect Logo

There are a lot of aspects that you need to consider when you design a logo and they include the font you use, the tagline, designs, colors and more.

When you are designing a logo for social media, there are a couple of different variables that you need to keep in mind. Also, even if you create a perfect logo, your work doesn't end there.

Creating a good logo is one of the steps of online marketing and your work as a marketer has only just begun. In this section, you will learn about certain tips that will help create a logo that will give you an attractive online presence.

The first thing that you need to consider is the aspect ratio.

You might or might not be able to use your logo as is. A couple of social media sites require you to convert your logo to a square or reduce its measurements to a square-shaped thumbnail. It doesn't mean that your logo needs to be perfectly square, but it must have the flexibility of being easily converted into one. Your logo must be able to fit into a small space, so avoid using a lot of unnecessary space while creating a logo.

Once you select a logo, you need to consistently use the same logo on all social media platforms. An effective social media marketing strategy includes different social networking platforms and your logo will be featured on multiple platforms. Therefore, use the same logo on all platforms. Consistency will impact the way your audience perceives your brand. If they see different logos on different platforms, it will confuse them, and they might not be able to recognize your brand.

While designing the logo, you can use detached text and graphics. You need to make sure that the text and graphics you use are separate components of the logo. This will come in handy when you need to convert your logo into a different size. In fact, a lot of brands and companies tend to use a single letter or a graphic in social media to ease its conversion.

Simplicity matters a lot. Further, it also poses the risk of the logo or some of its elements becoming unrecognizable when you resize the logo.

Keeping this in mind, it is a good idea to avoid long taglines, thin lines and intricately detailed graphics when you design a logo. Try to limit the colors and shades you use. A logo created with two or three colors works better on social media because it stands out and is visible in the crowd. If you think you don't possess the necessary skills to design a logo, you can always hire a graphic designer to help you.

When it comes to the overall success of your marketing campaign on Instagram, your logo is one thing that you cannot ignore. It helps create an identity for your brand. Even if a logo is a small aspect of a social media marketing campaign, it is a vital aspect that you cannot overlook.

## Instagram Bio

It is important that you understand the different components that comprise your Instagram bio. Once you do this, you can add more details and improve your account to ensure that the users understand what your brand is all about and what they can expect when they follow you.

The main problem that you face when you compose a bio is the little space you have. The Instagram section for the bio allows only 150 characters. Your username must fit under 30 characters.

With over 800 million users active on the app, you need to optimize all your chances of being discovered and follow an effective marketing strategy. In this section, you will learn about the different things you need to keep in mind to create a brilliant Instagram bio.

## The Profile Picture

Your Instagram profile page needs to include a profile photo relevant to your business or brand. The photo you use can be a logo or it can be a product photo.

Whatever you select as your profile photo, it needs to be attractive and the viewer must be able to easily associate it with your business. Usually a lot of companies, celebrities, brands and influencers use a verified badge on their profile photo to identify themselves.

One feature of Instagram is that it crops the uploaded profile picture into a circle. It means that your profile photo will be visible, and you need to be careful to make sure that it stays clear and visible even after cropping. You don't have to worry about uploading a photo with a square shape featuring your brand photo or logo right at the center. After all, the corners will be cut off without cutting off your branding.

## Username and Name

The username and the name are searchable in Instagram's search field. The username appears at the top of your Instagram profile and it will be quite prominent, and it will appear in bold text. Like mentioned earlier, it is important that you carefully select a username and a name.

If you have a simple and a short name, then the search results will show your profile easily. After the search, the name will appear in gray right below the profile's handle.

## Public Profile

You need to make sure that your Instagram handle is public and not private.

You will be shooting yourself in the leg if your profile is set as a private account. If your profile is a private account, then all those who visit your profile will not be able to view any of the photos you post.

It will act as an immediate deterrent and will prevent people from following you. To prevent all this, you simply need to make sure that you go to your account's settings and turn off the "Private Account" setting. If you have a business profile on Instagram, by default it will be a public account.

## Bio

The bio includes a short description and a synopsis of what you and your business are all about. A lot of companies use this space to list the products or services they offer, their website's URL, their location and their physical address. You need to keep the bio short because you only have 150 characters to convey all that you want to.

## Website

In the bio, you can include your website's URL to increase the visibility of your business and it also encourages those who visit your profile to visit the business website for more information. In this field, ensure you add a link to your website and don't skip it. After all, you need a landing page where you can direct all the traffic.

## Category

This is a feature that is only available for a business account. This category appears below a company's name and is directly linked to the one selected on the related Facebook page. For instance, indicating that you are in the restaurant business or a public figure is as easy as selecting the appropriate category.

## Call-to-Action Buttons

To activate the call-to-action buttons you need to fill out the necessary information that includes your email address, phone number and location. Previously, business account users used to write their email addresses and location address in the bio section.

This feature has been added for business account set up to free up some space in the bio section. Keep in mind that this feature is only shown in the app view and not the web view. You can find this feature by going to the Edit profile option and then select Contact Options.

## Email

When you add an email address to the bio, it creates an email button on your profile. Whenever someone clicks on the email option, the app promptly opens their default email app on their device. It makes it easier for your followers and potential customers to communicate with you through email.

## Directions

If you want to give your location, this is the field where you need to enter your physical address and help customers locate you easily. When a customer clicks on this button, it will prompt them to the default map application on their device.

## Call

Perhaps the best and the most convenient contact information is to add your business phone number. Using a phone call to communicate is the most personal form of communication. Whenever someone clicks on the call button, they will be prompted to use their default call application to make a call.

Recently, Instagram also released a new feature that allows you to use hashtags and profile links in the bio. It opens up a wide range of possibilities for marketers to use hashtags. For instance, if your brand has different Instagram handles for different aspects of your business; you can include a link to your other handles in your bio instead of making your followers search for them. It certainly makes it easier for people to find your handles especially when your accounts are not yet verified.

You can increase your visibility and relevance once you understand the ways in which you can optimally use the different components of your bio. A good bio will make more sense to your followers.

## How to Write the Bio

An Instagram bio tells the followers and other Instagrammers about the nature of your business. Essentially, it is a short description of yourself.

To make an impression, the bio needs to be concise and catchy. A catchy bio can lure people into following you and make them want to do business with you. If Instagram marketing is your main objective, ensure that you come up with a killer bio. Here are a couple of things that you need to keep in mind to create a brilliant bio.

## Include a Tagline

If you want to make your bio fascinating, use a tagline. A tagline will tell the viewers what your business is all about in a couple of words. Similarly, you can also use a summary of your company's values or add a mission statement to your bio.

## Be Minimalistic

A perfect Instagram bio is always short and simple. You need to provide all that information that your targeted customers will need to recognize the primary objective of your brand. You don't have to fill your bio with a lot of information, just stick to the essential components. After all, a visitor can browse through your Instagram posts or visit your website to find out more about your business.

## Link Your Account

It will make your bio efficient and will keep it to the point. You can link your Instagram account with your accounts on Facebook, Twitter, and Snapchat will allow your followers to easily find your company on other social media platforms. It increases your reach and increases your online visibility.

## A Branded Hashtag

A branded hashtag allows other Instagram users to share their content for you on their feed. A user can use your hashtag and this improves the scope of interacting with your audience. It also helps create a convincing brand story. If you have a branded hashtag, you need to include it in your bio.

Branded hashtags aren't restricted to just products and you can obtain one even for the services you provide. For instance, service provided could combine an emoji and a branded hashtag to set up a feed that will humanize their brand and make it seem more engaging. You need to remember that the clickable hashtags are only in the Instagram web interface and not on the mobile app.

## Use Emojis

Using emojis can really go a long way in helping a user to convey the personality and identity of a brand. Emojis can be used as an alternate for certain words and you can free up some space in your bio. Emojis also make Instagram posts and bio appear more exciting.

Emojis are quite cute and you might want to use them a lot, but it is a good idea to incorporate them in the Instagram bio toolbox. From faces to animals to other symbols, whichever emoji you choose will create a sense of brand personality.

An emoji can be worth a thousand words and will help you tell more about your brand than words can. In fact, you can effectively communicate using emojis and reduce the words you use. It will also help free up some space in your bio. Emojis are nice and have a certain appeal to them, but you need to remember that you must not go overboard with the emoji. Don't fill up your bio with emojis. After all, the viewers are not there to play Pictionary.

## Use Line Breaks

Using line breaks in an Instagram bio serves as a clear illustration of your proficiency in Instagram and its features. Even more, it makes a profile look more engaging and consumable.

## Include a Call-to-Action

When creating a perfect bio, keep in mind that you cannot avoid a proper call to action. Without a call-to-action, your bio is incomplete. The call to action must drive your targeted audience to visit your online store, access your website, call or email you for more information. Ask yourself what exactly you want visitors to do after viewing your profile before you decide a call-to-action.

## Include Contact Information

Providing a contact in your bio is very essential. Just imagine having a follower who is impressed by your business and wants to get in touch with you but does not have the contact.

This requires the need to include your contact information in your bio. It may be a phone number or an email address. Rather than just leaving a comment in the posts, users can reach out to you directly.

## What Makes You Unique?

What makes you unique compared to your competitors? State it in your bio and you will see the impact. Notably, customers want to get the best there is in the market and preferably from the most unique seller. When marketing, clearly indicate what makes you the best in your line of work.

A good Instagram profile must accurately describe what the business is about and what it can perfectly deliver. Provide unique skills and services to lure potential clients into not only following you but also to buy and make consecutive purchases from your business.

Include other fun facts about your brand because it is a great way to showcase the company's personality.

Keep all these steps in mind and you can easily create an interesting and engaging Instagram bio in no time. The one thing you must never forget while creating a bio is the character limit placed on it.

# CHAPTER 5

# GROW YOUR INSTAGRAM FOLLOWING

Attracting more followers on your Instagram profile can mean a stronger community for your brand, more traffic back to your website, and more sales for your business. But despite curating high-quality images and posting well-written posts, there is no guarantee that content alone can attract the right audience for your business.

In this chapter, we will explore the different tactics in making sure that your Instagram profile will gain a massive following.

## Be Faithful to Your Content Strategy

Ideally, your target followers should get a good idea of what your brand is really all about within a few seconds of visiting your profile. Your posts should tell you what you really care for and what you could offer for your audience who are looking for the same images in their feeds in the future.

When we follow a specific profile on Instagram, we already have established our expectations based on our interests and passion. If you follow an account and you see a lot of nice jewelry, you are expecting to see more of it along with other cool ways to pair these aesthetics with fashionable dresses. If you follow a profile with a lot of travel pictures, you might expect to see more of it along with great recommendations for tourist spots. Now try to imagine following a boho profile and then all of a sudden they share gothic images. That is a total mismatch. There's a big chance that you may unfollow that profile.

Likewise, if your target audience follows you, they are expecting to see more of what you are posting on your profile. So if your visual voice talks about vintage fashion, keep the vintage purses, chiffon dresses, and pearls coming. This doesn't mean you can't curate images of other things, but if vintage fashion is your niche, be faithful to it and create content revolving this topic. Posting punk fashion may disappoint your target audience who are expecting a more classic and sophisticated style. Your target audience must easily be able to know your posts when they see it in their feeds.

## Use the Power of Hashtags

Using hashtags is a great tactic you can use to make certain that your content will reach people who may likely follow you. And with the volume of images being uploaded every day to the platform, you really need to use hashtags for your niche so you can stand out. Generic hashtags such as #fashion #style #love are very popular so your posts may easily get lost in the millions of photos with the same hashtag. The key is to really find the right hashtags for your brand.

To do this, you have to take some time to see the types of hashtags being used by leading profiles in your niche. Obviously, Instagram profiles with good following are using specific strategies that bring great visibility. If you found specific hashtags, determine the number of posts for each hashtag (including the top 9 grid).

For example, Coca Cola's #shareacoke campaign was among the best practices in Instagram marketing. Same with Calvin Klein's #MyCalvins.

You can add 30 hashtags on Instagram posts, and it is ideal if you could maximize this space. But there are instances when the hashtags could clutter the caption. As a workaround, you can add them as a comment. Just make sure to use '. . . . .' or a dot for every line so the comment will be truncated.

Adding hashtags can be time-consuming, so another tactic you can use is to save the hashtags you normally use into different categories so that you can just copy the right set of hashtags you want to include.

It is best to use a combination of niche and popular hashtags. If you use niche types with fewer images, there's a big chance that they will be featured in the top 9 grid, which will greatly help your brand to be discovered and attract more followers.

Join the Instagram Stories Bandwagon

Instagram Stories is one of the most effective tools for attracting a massive following. This will provide your followers a sneak peek into your brand, the people behind your team, and it also increases engagement to record heights. Instagrammers like to see raw and real posts, so be sure to post stories that are not too formal or salesy without compromising your content strategy.

Another great thing about using Instagram Stories is that you can gain an advantage if your stories are featured in the Explore Tab (the stories that you can see at the top of the page). These stories are selected by Instagram's algorithm based on the type of content that you often interact with. More often than not, these are the profiles that you don't follow, but still, they are posting the type of content that you are likely to engage with. Hence, if you have been viewing posts that are related to herbal medicine, you will see a lot of Stories featuring this niche.

When you make your stories really engaging and you regularly post high-quality content, Instagram will often feature you in the Explore tab. This may bring you a lot of followers!

## Engagement Over Volume

In any social media channel, the volume of your followers will be useless if the engagement is low. You should set your strategy in a way that it will encourage your followers to interact with your content.

The quality of your followers is a crucial element in Instagram marketing. A brand with 1,000 followers who are regularly engaging with your content is far more valuable compared to a brand with 100,000 random followers composed of people who are not all qualified to be your target audience. You should attract followers who can resonate with your posts, so they can share them and interact with your online community.

In addition, the reach of your audience is an important element to consider—more than the number of your followers. For instance, even if you only have 1,000 followers on Instagram, you can gain a bigger audience if the majority of these followers are influencers in the social network.

Use the Recommended Image Size for Instagram

Using the ideal size for your Instagram images will substantially improve the aesthetic appeal of your feed, which could translate to more followers. Take note that the standard image size for Instagram is 1080 px by 1080 px. This is different from the previous standard Instagram post of 612 px by 612 px.

Instagram had to upgrade its platform so the app could keep up with high-resolution displays for advanced handheld devices. Aside from using the ideal size, you should also make certain that your posts are visually appealing. Studies suggest that brighter images attract 600 percent more likes compared to those with darker filters. Interestingly, muted palettes also tend to attract more likes, so you must use grays, blues, and greens.

## Hold Instagram Promos

Holding Instagram-exclusive promos, contests, and events can significantly boost not only the number of your followers but also your engagement. Despite the many advances in the modern world, customers are still attracted to freebies and giveaways.

Just be sure that your promos will result in more followers or could improve engagement. In addition, your promo mechanics should be clear, and you should be specific on how you want your followers to participate in the promo.

## Below are some examples of contests on Instagram:

Tag friends - Your followers can qualify to participate in the contest if they tag two or three of their Instagram friends in the comment area of the contest picture

Hashtag contests - Your audience can share their own pictures by adding a contest-centric hashtag to the picture to become eligible for the contest.

Liking and commenting - Followers can qualify for the contest just by liking the photo specified for the contest

If you also want to increase brand awareness, you may offer your product as the prize. Also, remember to use a hashtag when you are holding a contest so that you can easily monitor the progress of the event.

As a recap, you can do the following to increase the number of your Instagram followers:

- Develop a solid content strategy and stick to it

- Embrace the power of hashtags (be sure to combine niche and popular ones)

- Maximize your exposure with Instagram Stories

- Prioritize follower engagement and quality over volume

- Use the current standard image size for your pictures (1080 px by 1080 px)

- Hold Instagram-exclusive contests

# CHAPTER 6

# INSTAGRAM CONTENTS

As stated earlier, Instagram is a platform that works by visuals posts. Everything shared are either photos, graphics or videos. Because of this, very many people find it hard to create contents; many don't even know how to post or whether a posting is allowed. Those that know these are confused on what sort of content should be on Instagram. In this section, you will be taken through the parts of the content, types of contents and processes of creating content on Instagram. Attention is paid keenly to direct you through crafting perfect posts.

Because of the nature of the platform, visuals and branded storytelling are the keys of contents used. To engage your followers as a business-oriented person, telling a story about your product and services is the key to being the best seller. Posting pictures that are 'meaningless' will never add anything to your account. On Instagram, create a story that will be of great impact to your followers and any potential ones. The best thing to do is to put your gaze on your followers. You must, with utmost clarity, put them into consideration because they are the one to be engaged. Be adroit in your post to ensure entertainment and genuine contents. Be skillful in the way you arrange your photos. While uploading the photos, show them the nature of people in support of your business, the type of person you are, the muse of your story, and lots more. Don't take the time of your audience; make the story succinct and exclusive to Instagram news only. Be dynamic in the chronological arrangement of the stories. To ensure uniqueness of your profile, make sure you are updated on the latest trends on the platform. These trends could be news or hashtags, write on them and use them as well. Devise a way of connecting your interesting contents in such a way that your followers will have to stay on your profile to get the full story. Get the interaction with them interesting; they will surely look up for more. There are some basic things to consider while constructing a good Instagram content. These, according to Martins, are:

## The Right time

You have to skillfully detect the right time to post your story based on your targeted audience. You must be up-to-date on their personal activities. Note that on your newsfeed, the most recent posts receive more attention which is why your post must be timely. You must key into an opportunity such as this. According to Martin "if your viral page is aimed at students who are online in the morning, then you should post in this period." This means the free time which your targeted audience is likely to be free to check their Instagram should be considered before posting. He gave another example that if you have 9-to5-jobbers as a target group, then you should write more posts after work. These people will have free time randomly; by this, you must post in their timing too. He, however, gave a recommendation which is not 'convenient test' as generally 7-9 clock (breakfast), 11-14 clock (lunch) and 17 to 20 clock (after work). The best interaction on Instagram was also given as 17-18 clock. The time frame of your location should not affect your audience consideration. Although most times, you and your followers are in the same meridian.

## The Picture

Instagram can also be referred to as an electronic photo album. This is because it contains much of them. The pictures to be posted must be very attractive. Consider editing your photos before uploading them. Make sure the post is dynamic with different types of things such as comedy videos, photos and all. Try to upload pictures that are showing the practical time people are consuming your product. Research has it that many people consider photos from real life scenes of the product as the authenticity of the product. High-quality photos are recommended; make sure you don't post low-quality photos and videos. Be dynamic in the selection and arrangement of the pictures. Make sure you include a brand of your company on a photo that is not really related. Don't let your followers have bad impressions about you. If you make necklaces, consider using your friends as part of the models and then take their pictures for onward uploads on to your account. Take pictures of people that have worn the necklace to events such as weddings to authenticate it. Being outstanding should be your goal by creating compelling contents that entertain people. The type of pictures you will post for children will be different from the adults'. You must do all your best to get their target at different times as well. You should catch their attention at once sometimes too. The arrangement of your pictures also matters. The recommended arrangement is the grid formula. With a grid, you have the opportunity to arrange your pictures chronologically to explain the story you are telling. Apart from this, followers can quickly trace the story effortlessly. The posts must be able to hold anyone that runs across the posts; they must locate your account and follow.

## The Text

Even though Instagram is basically visual, texts could be added to it sometimes too. Most times, these texts should be one that will require the action of the followers. The texts should vary between lengthy words and short ones. The place your company is located will be an additional text for you in cases you don't know the text to use. The aim is to engage your followers. Your text must be relevant to your pictures and most times should be one or two words. When you include your location, the post will be expanded to reach more audience thereby popularizing the account –this is your goal. Make sure the text is proofread, don't spoil the mind of the people that are already interested in you. Text can be a statement on the images uploaded as well. With this, if you are uploading pictures that are not a direct replica of your product, many of your followers will understand vividly.

## Best steps to creating audience-centered contents

Having a business account requires the consistent engagement of your audience. This makes good contents an unavoidable thing to be included in your profile. You can consider the following tricks given by Instagram influencer Christina Galbato when creating a laudable content:

## Use ready-made templates tools

When you want to create contents on Instagram and wonder how to create a pattern for them or perhaps stumbled on a great profile with nice and cool contents, and you want to create, template tools is what top Instagram influencers used. There are lots of tools Canva, Venngage and Adobe with great Spark posts. These tools will craft an outstanding content that titillates the eyes and leave the mind wondering what sort the pictures is. You don't need to stress yourself, search for any of these tools, insert your pictures and you will be wowed by the outcome. It has trial sections, and you can equally choose manually that template you love.

## Research and Use High-quality stock images

That you will need lots of images is a fact. On the contrary, stock images could be awkward on your news-feed. Be extremely careful while using it most especially with templates. Everyone needs varying images to be created as contents, visit Stocksnap.io or Unsplash for free nice images. If you are buoyant enough, you could log onto Stocksy for images with high quality, different niche pictures, etc. Stocksy provides the greatest images because it is paid for and the developers want it to be worth it. Bear in mind that the standard pixel for images to be uploaded as content on Instagram is 1080p X 1080p to avoid automatic image resolutions. Stock images are always great and nice because the sites where they are found were actually developed to meet the criteria of social platforms such as Instagram.

## Vary your content's format

Dynamism is the way forward in having a good followers' turn up on your content. You can't be deaf to the reaction of the followers when creating your contents. You could create a short video, say of 1-minute duration, explaining your product or showing the practical usage of your product. Don't bore your viewers with just a single type of pictures; it could be extremely boring really. A good Instagram profile will house varying contents. The distinction in the contents is only in their format. Take your time to create GIF contents as well. You could have a picture, GIF and short video and their permutation as well. This is what your audience is expecting, give them. Though Instagram takes both GIF and Videos as the same thing, GIF is always shorter but interactive. Lots of people expect it as well. Stuff your contents with a variety of formats.

Search for brands within your niche and repost them

Perhaps creating contents yourself is barely possible because of time constraints. Don't worry; there is a way out of the tunnel. You can, with the consent of the writer, report a post within your niche from another content writer. Example of posts you could repost are those posts from fast-growing Instagram users. They must be of interest to your audience though. However, on Instagram, there are special steps to go through in order to make reposting official —reposting without proper consultation could lead to offense. Follow the steps below:

## 1. Follow hashtags and accounts to find out quality content

In order to validate your reposting, ensure that you have a similar audience and brand. Make the person you want repost his/her content is not a direct competitor to you. Make sure you have proper thinking on the content as well. You must follow the person in order to be updated on the posts of the person. To save the contents you would love to repost, try to create a collection for easy access. Searching for related contents through hashtag is also a legal way.

## 2. Contact the user for permission to repost

Before asking for permission, make sure you let the writer know they are doing a great job with proper credit and that your audience will be interested in the same post. To ask for permission, send the writer a DM through the arrow beneath the picture. Using the arrow has proven most efficient way, according to the report, of sending a direct message to account users.

## 3. Share the picture on your news feed

You can now share the picture to your feed once the permission has been granted. You must make sure proper credit is given to the source of the post anyway.

## 4. Save the Photo from Instagram or share directly through the repost feature

There are two ways of reposting on Instagram: saving from Instagram and reposting directly. For the first one, you will need to find the picture, click on the photo, double click it, view page source, type jpg there, copy the URL of the first option, open a new browser, paste it there, right click and save the picture. On the second option, copy the URL of the post you like and click on "repost" and it will automatically repost it. Note that the watermark is maintained when you use the second option. The first looks complex likewise, try to accompany the process given with required practical.

## Create a UGC Campaign

The acronym UGC means 'User Generated Content.' It is used as content created by your followers. You could be the initiator, and they could post within your niche. This is also an activity similar to reposting of contents. User-generated content is typically contents crafted by any product user on their products without encouragement from anyone. These are contents solicited by you from your followers, though most times with incentives to encourage them. You can involve your followers in different ways: selling your product at a discount rate, conducting a competition on creating a post on your brand, etc. Instagram has suggested that you announce your hashtag even on other platforms especially the part of the incentives. Be strategic and dynamic in your request for contents from your audience. Without dynamism in your request, your feed will always be the same thing which will bore your audience. If you stipulate too many rules are guiding the kind of post you want, you might end up with no post as many people might be afraid they won't be considered. Relying too much on your followers is not a good idea as well. Make sure their posts are just supplementary and not the main thing. Proof to them you can actually create your content yourself and create a feeling that their support is a means to encourage them only.

## Do influencer collaboration

One fantastic thing to do to create a good audience-centered profile is to work with other great brand promoters too. This will get you new followers, great feed and many other things enjoyed by the person you collaborated with. You must ensure the collaboration is with someone within your own niche to avoid exploitation and misunderstanding. Worry less on how to contact top influencers as many of them have a contact in their bio basically for collaboration inquiries purpose.

You have learned how to create good content for your brand and business. However, note that whatever means you are using to get your contents, designing will surely be done by you. Because of this, you will need to learn basic tricks used by top influencers to design their contents. These tricks are:

✓ **Stating a precise focal point**

While uploading your pictures and creating your format, make sure your photo has focus. The focus of photos means the center where you want your viewers to pay their attention only. If you create a picture with lots of images on, you might lose the focus, affecting its effect on the viewers. Therefore, put a single image with many other things, if need be, pointing only to the central idea of the photo.

✓ **Adhere to the rule of thirds**

The rule of thirds, found in photography, is all about arranging your interesting features along with a 9-grid picture intersection. This rule is a classic rule and executed by 9-grid photo imagination. Make sure that in uploading many pictures on your profile, you must adhere strictly to this rule –it is the secret of the top influencers. With amazing third rule obedience, you will adjust your grid to one-third of the picture you wish to upload as well.

✓ **Create and apply white space and borders**

Creating space and borders around your photos gives it a compelling look, and the audience will always want to gaze more. To avoid jam-packed uploads, ensure that you maintain some space between your third rule and focal point picture. Make sure you add this effect to all your posts, and you will experience rapid growth of followers.

✓ **Rapt attention should be to Contrast and balance**

Give your picture a good contrast while uploading. The contrast of your picture ranges over its color, light, shape, fonts, white space and border, and lots more. To ensure you have a perfect contrast setting, you could play around the various types of it on your Instagram app. Contrast is an important part of content designed to highly engage your audience. Many people are fascinated by the enhancement of a given picture even before focusing on the content itself. Contrast is like a finishing effect that 'crowns' your effort in content design. This is the last stage of content design, make sure it counts, and you will be amazed by the number of turn out your account will experience.

# CHAPTER 7

# INSTAGRAM HACKS FOR TAKING REALLY GOOD PHOTOS

If you couldn't get this until now, Instagram is a great place to market your business. The photo sharing platform has all the right tools for promoting your brand. However, since the majority of the posts on this platform are photos, how can you stand out among the tough competition out there?

The answer to this is by using good photos for your posts. Making your photos attractive and of the best quality gives you the edge you need to help boost your page.

It is true that your photos must be top-notch but the question is how can you take great photos that will be of the best quality?

Here are some tips that will help you take the best photos:

## 1. Plan ahead

Planning ahead before taking the picture is a good way to start the process of taking good photos. You are advised to think about your brand and what you really want to offer your audience. Advanced planning gives you a good idea about what you want to do. That will give you a blueprint to work with.

## 2. Don't be obsessed with people's thoughts

When you are through with your plan, take the time to find you what you really like. Your thoughts shouldn't be focused primarily on what the Instagram community wants from you, or the type of photo is the most popular amongst the members of the community. If you give heed to these thoughts, you will defeat your goal of getting the best picture before you even took out the camera.

## 3. Use natural sources of light

One of the most important factors you must consider is lighting. It is the key to the overall beauty of your photos. Note that even the best photo-editing app with the most complex filter can never make a good job of a poorly-lit photo. Using natural sources of light will give your photos the right illumination. If you must take any photo outdoors, you should consider doing so early in the morning, late in the afternoon, or overcast days. These periods are when you can get the best shots.

## 4. Use your eyes before your camera

Your eyes still remain an important and efficient tool for taking good photos. It is customary to see people taking a couple of pictures, comparing them, and then making their choice. Instead of towing that path and wasting time taking tens of shots before settling for the best, use your eyes before using the camera.

This requires that you look at the object critically, frame the picture with your eyes, and observe the object for some time. This may give you a new perspective for looking at the object so that you can get the best shot after taking a few pictures.

## 5. Use the grid feature

It is good to bring your composition in when attempting to take a picture. Whenever you want to take a picture, you can make the best job of it by turning on the grid. You can watch the elements overlapping through your viewfinder or on the screen until you get the perfect conditions for shooting. That will enhance the beauty of your photo.

## 6. Use the point of interest

A common feature of all good photos is the presence of a point of interest. It may be someone in the foreground or a great landscape with sharp lines that focuses the viewer's eyes. Great photos are known for having more than one point of interest without them overlapping and creating a sense of clutter. Try to let your photo reveal a little information about the place or person. Let it tell a story about the point of interest.

## 7. Watch out for moments

Another way to make your photo great is by letting your pictures have great moments. Let the moments be about the subjects or subject you want to shoot. Look for some natural moments such as extreme, peak, settled, or emotional moments. Either of these moments will make the picture interesting.

If there are unwanted pieces of information, stay away from them. The unwanted information may detract from the great moment and impact the picture negatively. You can only be pardoned if the unwanted information contributes to the overall beauty of the image.

Your goal is to have a clean image, free of unwanted clutter, that draws the attention of the viewers directly to the story you want to tell.

## 8. Strong shapes, colors, and lines are good

One of the qualities of a good Instagram image is strong colors and well-defined lines. The photo should contain some elements that will loom large in your camera's frame so that it can easily draw the attention of the viewers. Through personal training and regular practice, you will develop the skills for conveying some emotions with your pictures.

## 9. Use third-party apps

There are tons of third-party apps that you can use to make your pictures stand out. These apps come in different forms and for a wide variety of functions. You can explore the functionalities of these apps to add to the overall beauty of your images.

An app that is good for simulating a slow shutter to some moving objects, such as blurry water, can create a long-exposure effect. The effect will be more pronounced on waterfalls or incredibly large bodies of water. That will give you the perfect condition to show high contrast between the sharp, still surroundings and the water.

## 10. Use light from strange sources

If you compare your phone camera with traditional cameras, you will see a clear distinction. The lens of the phone camera has a different way of absorbing light than the camera. That makes it possible for the phone camera to see light from some strange places such as behind the object or above it.

If you move the object around without taking your eyes off it through your phone camera, you will see the object as it transforms until you can see the rays of light on your lens. The light will have a powerful impact on the image. This is the moment you are waiting for. Take your shot right here.

## 11. Leverage the burst mode

When taking a picture, you may see the need to make a moment stand still without losing its detail. If you want to do that, shoot in daylight or in a well-lit space so that you can use a fast shutter speed.

Ensure that you tap the screen to make it possible to lock focus on the object manually. You can also make the exposure perfect by using the slide bar before taking the shot. With burst mode, you have a perfect tool that will be useful when choosing the most appropriate moment for the picture.

## 12. Shoot from a wide variety of angles

You can try to take your pictures from viewpoints that look quite unusual. If you consider a view to be normal, it can actually look awesome if you shoot it from a different perspective than through the perspective you see.

Consider shooting from as many angles as possible to make your pictures more appealing. You can try the right-down or up-high position and see the impact it has on your image.

## 13. Use props

You should consider using different objects, and observe their impact on the story you are trying to tell. By taking your environment and the background of the object into consideration, you can do a good job of making your photo look great by making the scene come alive.

## 14. Use a bad weather to your advantage

While some people curl up at the idea of having to deal with bad weather while shooting, you can use the bad weather to your advantage. Whenever there is fog, snow, or rain you should go out there and find a way to make the best use of that weather to shoot a unique picture. An experienced photographer once suggested that you should use bad weather to make good photographs.

## 15. Use the puddles after the rain

After a rainfall, go out there and take awesome photos. The puddles will give you reflections that you can utilize to contribute beauty to your pictures. That background will be great for taking interesting pictures and you shouldn't hesitate to use them.

## 16. Consider using white space

White space is fun to use. They add uniqueness and beauty to your picture. Take a look at some masterpieces like the latest catalog of J.Crew, or an outstandingly beautiful home. What common feature do they have? Both of these use tons of white space.

You can imitate them and bring such an impression to your picture so that you can make your Instagram feed neat and clutter free. How you feel about those pictures when you see them mirrors the way others will feel when viewing your Instagram feed when it has enough white space.

The best way to have a good shot with white space is to look for white backgrounds when shooting. If you want to photograph a person, you can shoot in front of a white wall to have that effect on your picture.

If you want to shoot an object, a white window sill or a piece of foam board should be used for photographing the object in order to add the white space effect.

Some font apps also have such feature. You can try WordSwag and use it to put an impressive quote on your photo to give it that white space effect. That will give your feed some breathing room.

## 17. Take advantage of the portrait mode

Instagram has a new portrait mode that you can take advantage of. You can use it to lay emphasis on the length of a particular scene. You can also use it to tell a detailed story that just isn't possible with a square crop.

## 18. Add more elements

Adding more elements to your scale will make your photo look great. Adding scale to your image can be done by simply including a person in the image's frame. You can try different poses within the same scene to find the best one that will add to the beauty of your image.

## 19. Layers are handy

Using layers for your images makes it possible to convey a perfect message to the viewer. The goal is to let the viewers share the same point of view with you. Using these will give your audience a good view of your brand because they see your brand exactly the way you want them to see it.

## 20. Use patches of light

You can find patches of light in different places. The street lamp and the rays of sunlight are perfect sources for these patches of light. During a photography session, find them and use them to enhance your skills.

An important attribute of using patches of light emanating from the sun is that the patches will always give you a variety of backgrounds to use. Make use of that to give your audience a perfect picture.

## 21. Use the dusk to your advantage

Even when the sun is going down you can still stay out to take beautiful pictures. Although we have limited vision when the sun goes down, modern cameras have better ability to pick up light than humans.

This is a good way to give your audience something beautiful. By leveraging the unusual power of the camera to capture the captivating moments of a sunset, you can give your audience something truly amazing.

## 22. Move as physically possible to your subject

You can get more than you bargain for if you can move closer to your object as much as possible. Whether you want to shoot animals or people, it is advisable that you get close to them. That creates the right emotion and intimacy in your work. Your audience will appreciate the output and the sense of intimacy associated with the picture. Move closer to the object and use the widest focal length you can. That will bring the object into perspective, and will fill the frame of the photo. The result is a subject that is popped out so much that this cannot be achieved without the lens.

If you are an iPhone user, Moment has a good wide angle lens that will give you the best results. On the other hand, DSLR users may find the 16-35 mm lens very useful.

## 23. Use your phone's accessories

When considering taking a good shot, a lens attachment can make all the difference in improving your photo. If you want to add some character to the photo, consider using a wide angle lens.

## 24. Your edits should be simple

The availability of different editing tools has turned some people into editing freaks. While some people keep their edits simple, some have a tendency over edit their shots. Experience has shown that over-edited photos can lose its appeal. Therefore, when using filters to give your photos the best look, resist the urge to overdo it.

Whichever editing tool you use, be moderate. Don't push a photo too far from its real natural state. Users won't find it attractive that way. However, subtle tweaks are cool and will help the image to maintain its natural look.

A study by the social media scientist at HubSpot, Dan Zarella, revealed that photos that don't have too much color saturation in them get more likes than the others that are over-edited. What else did the stats say? Such images can get almost 600% likes more than other posts.

## 25. Always aim for quality

You can up your game on Instagram by curating your feed and making sharing a better part of your activities as opposed to posting. The implication here is that you should be selective about lighting and composition. That will give you tons of high-quality images to choose from to share with your audience.

## 26. Make practice a way of life

You can't get it right at your first attempt. You need tons of hours of regular practice sessions to master the art of taking beautiful pictures. If you have the time to make regular practices, you will gradually know your tools and the best ways to take amazing shots.

Always be ready to get a good shot whenever an interesting scene, location, moment, or light pops up. Cultivate the habit of doing a good job composing good photos. You can also take a couple of frames of the same object to get the best results while you also pay close attention to the editing.

The results will be sharp, clean photos that will wow you with natural colors and appealing tones.

The hours of practice sessions will be fully rewarding as the appreciation for your posts increase, and as more followers join your base.

# CHAPTER 8

# HOW TO USE STORYTELLING ON INSTAGRAM

Now that you have created your Instagram page and have also started communicating with your followers on Instagram, the next thing you need to focus on is to come up with ways in which you can reach a wider audience. Essentially, it is all about understanding how you can create a huge fan base for yourself without being someone famous outside the Instagram community.

If you use Instagram for marketing, then you might have noticed a dip in the number of followers you have at some point or the other. Don't worry about this. It might happen that you aren't receiving as many likes, comments or new followers like you did in the past. In any case, it isn't just you who hits a snag like this. In this section, you will learn about different ways in which you can become a compelling storyteller and increase your reach. In this section, you will learn about the ways in which you can become a better storyteller by understanding your audience.

Select A Theme

You need to select a theme for your Instagram page that will appeal to your niche. It is not just about selecting a theme, but you need to stick to it as well.

What's even better is that if you can make a unique name for yourself. If you want users on Instagram to follow you, then you need to publish consistent and high-quality content frequently. If they know that they can count on your page for this, they will want to follow you.

Join Instagram Engagement Groups

Are you trying to figure out how to increase your followers on

Instagram? If yes, then you need to join Instagram engagement groups. It might be difficult to make your way into the biggest Instagram engagement groups, you will certainly get a list of more targeted Instagram followers by sticking to your niche. It is quite easy to find Instagram engagement groups. If you are a member of such a group, then it is quite easy to obtain followers and receive likes from those who have similar interests to you. If you are serious about increasing your visibility, then ensure that you return the favor and follow the fan pages for people who join the group.

Even if it may not help with immediate sales, it helps your brand gain goodwill. You need to understand that this strategy will work only in the short-term and is not effective in the long run.

Ask Customers to Share their Photos

You can always ask your customers to share their photos in your feed. In fact, it is a good strategy that you can use if you are just starting out with Instagram marketing. It also goes a long way in establishing social proof for your brand. If you haven't been doing great business, then reach out to your target audience and offer a free gift or any other incentive if they share quality images of the products you sell. Obviously, giving incentives is not a long-term strategy, but it certainly works for increasing short-term sales. It helps you grow as a brand. As more and more users start to see the content shared by customers, it naturally increases the interest in your brand.

Produce Content Your Audience Will Love

Whenever you are thinking about the type of content that is ideal for your business, you need to focus on ensuring that the posts are extraordinary. You need to create content that your audience will love. It isn't about you; it is about your audience. It might seem obvious, but content creation is one aspect of Instagram that a lot of people seem to neglect. You need to understand what your audience likes and you need to create content accordingly.

Regardless of what you decide to use, you need to be able to connect with your audience. When creating content, keep this age-old adage "beauty lies in the eyes of the beholder" in your mind. This is the reason why you need to establish a good relationship with your audience so that you can learn about the type of content that will appeal to them. There have been numerous occasions where people decided to post something that they thought their audience would like, but to their utter dismay, it turned out to be a dud.

One way in which you can produce great content is to check out the kind of content that your competition is posting. You also need to take a note of the imagery that they use. Also, never just copy and paste stuff.

Choosing the Right Instagram Content

If you want a huge following on Instagram, then you need to produce high-quality content. It must not only be tailor-made for your Instagram page, but must also be exactly what your target audience needs. When you are creating content, you need to find the right approach as well as the style. It is important because your content will be the way that your followers will recognize your business.

Negotiate to get Shoutouts

You will also want to know about the different ways in which you can obtain a greater number of followers. One of the simplest ways to do this is via shoutouts. If you decide to use this trend, then your page will gain a lot of popularity within a couple of weeks or even months.

Essentially, shoutouts are a form of advertising other pages, and are usually done by authority pages or influencers. Speaking in a general sense, a shoutout is when a famous Instagrammer or influencer mentions your page on their own account and then tells their followers to check your page and encourages them to follow you. Shoutout is a great way to get your name in front of a huge audience of potential followers.

Use Apps to Increase Instagram Followers

There are different apps that you can use to increase your Instagram followers. A lot of people tend to use a bot to achieve this purpose. In most cases, they are known as Instagress. It works quite well, at least initially, and allows users to gain their first couple of thousands of Instagram followers. Eventually, the popular handles stop using the bots since they aren't of any use after gaining the necessary following. Unfortunately, Instagress and other similar apps that are used to increase the number of followers are usually shut down after they are noticed by the administrators of the platform. It might seem tempting to use something like this, but it is better if you avoid it.

Repost Other's Content

There are some who entirely build their Instagram profiles based on reposting the content created by others. The only way in which you can successfully do this is by giving the necessary credit to the creator and by obtaining their permission before you go ahead and post their content. In fact, it is one of the policies of Instagram that you need to seek the permission of that specific content's creator before you use it.

Use Insights

It's quite easy to track your followers and post's impressions you receive on Instagram. One thing that you need to keep in mind if you want to gain more followers is to convert your Instagram page into a business page. Once you do this, you can use the information available on Insights to monitor the way your posts are doing. Not just this, there are several other metrics that you can monitor as well.

# CHAPTER 9

# FACTORS THAT AFFECT THE VISIBILITY OF YOUR INSTAGRAM POSTS

The visibility of your Instagram posts is determined by Instagram's algorithm. If you are a regular Facebook user, you may have heard about the Facebook News Feed algorithm. This algorithm combines mystery with ingenuity. The algorithm is responsible for the Facebook's showing of only the best content to Facebook users.

Therefore, users who are reputable for creating good content do enjoy great followers while non-followers can still see their posts on their news feed. Instagram adopts the same algorithm for its own operation. How does the Instagram algorithm work?

In this chapter, I will break down the mechanism of the Instagram algorithm so that you can become familiar with the factors that have an impact on how your content ranks on your followers' feeds. I will also go over how you can benefit from the Instagram algorithm if you are a marketer.

**Let me first address how the algorithm works.**

If you want a straightforward answer to how the algorithm works, the answer is, "It's complicated."

While a cloud of mystery surrounds Instagram's algorithm, there is sufficient information about it to have a glimpse of how it works. This is, nevertheless, not complete information about its mode of operation, but a simple idea.

From several studies, it was discovered that some key factors are considered when ranking content. As an Instagram user, especially if you are using it for business purposes, you should pay a close attention to these seven factors:

## 1. Engagement

Engagement refers to the degree of popularity of your posts. It is known that a post with a high degree of popularity will have better engagement than one with lower popularity. That explains the connection between the engagement and popularity of a post.

According to the CEO and founder of the popular social media analytics site Social Media Examiner, Michael Stelzner says that whenever you publish a post on behalf of your brand or yourself, the algorithm is designed to show the published post to a section of the target audience. The goal is to see the sample audience's reaction to the post in order to determine how far the post should go. If the response is impressive, it will be shown to the public. Otherwise, if the response is not encouraging, the post will be limited to the sample audience. What is the implication?

Any of you who post with a higher engagement has a better chance at ranking higher on your feed than those with lower engagement. Some of the factors that are considered as parts of engagement include video views, likes, share, comments, story views, saves, and live videos.

If someone you are following comments or likes a post, the algorithm will use the engagement to see whether you might be interested in the post too. As such, the algorithm is designed to show that post on your feed.

While this focuses on engagement, another point to consider is the relevance of your post to your brand.

## 2. Relevance

Your ranking is not determined by your posts alone, it takes another factor into consideration: the relevance your post has to your audience. Why is this important?

When launching the Instagram algorithmic timeline, the social media site announced that importance will be attached to relevance when showing content. So, you will be fed with the posts that you are interested in before any other post.

The Instagram management said that *"The order of your photos and videos in your feed will be based on the likelihood you'll be interested in the content, your relationship with the person posting, and the timeliness of the post."* You may wonder then, how does Instagram have an idea of what really interests you?

The answer to that question is simple. The algorithm goes through your conversations in the past and uses that information to predict your interests. For instance, if your engagement with fashion posts in the past outweighs that of any other topic, it will assume that your interest lies in fashion. Expectedly, your feed will be filled with fashion-related posts.

Although Instagram thrives on photos, the availability of complex photo recognition software makes it possible for the algorithm to classify posts into different genres. Another clue is the hashtags used with a post. They give a post away; making it easy for the algorithm to identify which posts are classified and where they are classified.

This rule also applies to your audience too.

## 3. Relationships

Your relationship refers to the accounts you have frequent interactions with. Instagram has put a measure in place to ensure that you don't miss the posts of those who are very close to you.

Since Facebook owns Instagram, it is expected that information from Facebook can be used to determine your schoolmates, friends, colleagues, family, and others you enjoy an intimate relationship with. Therefore, the algorithm is built to make provisions for you so that you won't miss the posts from your family and friends. As a result, the posts of these loved ones will rank higher on your feed than that of other people.

Another important factor that the Instagram algorithm uses is the history of your interactions in the past. This information is also used to determine who among your Facebook friends should be included amongst your loved ones and best friends.

While speaking about some of the factors that Instagram's algorithm considers, a software engineer at Instagram named Thomas Dimson mentioned the following group of people:

Those whose content you always like.

People you exchange direct messages with.

People you personally search for.

People with whom you have an offline relationship with.

If you have a steady interaction based on the criteria above, you have a good chance of having your close associates' posts on your feed. This is due to the algorithm that makes the assumption of what kinds of relationships you have with people.

Although this may not be the exact criteria Instagram uses for ranking, it still gives us a good idea of what may be going on behind the curtain. It shows that Instagram thinks you want to be kept in the loop with people you interact with regularly. Hence, their content will form a huge part of your feed.

## 4. Timeliness

The timeliness of your post also has a bearing on the post you wake up to see. This is a factor that measures how recent your posts are. It is common knowledge that older messages will rank lower while recent posts will fare better. Therefore, this practice is done to give you recent posts with the belief that you will be interested in them.

Instagram may then consider to feed you with posts that are published a couple of minutes ago as opposed to the ones that were published 3 days ago as part of its effort to give you the most current information.

This underlines the importance of recent posts and their naturalness to be found easily on your feed.

A study conducted recently gave insight into this. According to the study, the best time to publish your post is usually at the peak period of activity when competition is reduced to the bare minimum. It was suggested that the ideal time is usually between 9 am to 10 am.

So, having the knowledge of the best time you will get your followers to interact with your post is a good and convenient way to reach most of them so that you can sustain your relationship. This will of course lead to improved user engagement too.

## 5. Profile searches

If you check out certain accounts often, the Instagram algorithm will also consider that when factoring in how to disperse your posts to your followers. According to the algorithm, a regular search for a particular person or item considers the likelihood that you are interested in that brand or individual. To keep your interest alive, Instagram will do anything possible to ensure you always have posts from such people on your feed.

To spare you the stress of manually searching for the profile regularly, Instagram will try to rank the posts of such individuals or brands higher on your feed to increase your relationship with them rather than letting you take it upon yourself to do that. This will have a positive impact on your Instagram experience.

According to Thomas, the implementation of this algorithm led to a corresponding decrease in the number of searches on Instagram. This is a sign that since people can readily have posts from individuals they always search on their feed, the need to have to make a search for such individuals decreased.

## 6. Direct shares

One of the many appreciated features of Instagram is the ability to share a post you find attractive or informative for you. Direct Instagram post shares is another factor that plays a significant role when considering what posts should appear on your feed. The frequency at which you search someone's posts is another important factor for the Instagram algorithm. It uses that information to make a connection between you and that individual, based on how often you look them up and share their posts.

Instagram considers this in two different ways. First, Instagram considers sharing a post as an indication of interest in the account owner. The algorithm remembers this when ranking posts that will go into your feed.

Second, Instagram will take a look at people whose posts you share. It does that to establish a connection with you that can be explored in the future to determine what you get and what doesn't go into your feed.

When discussing relationships, Instagram considers it a sign of showing personal interest in someone if you share posts with them. So, the Instagram algorithm may rank the post of someone you share posts with on your feed.

## 7. Time spent

The time you spend on a post is a sign of your interest in the post. If the algorithm used for Facebook is used here, we can have a good idea of the relationship of time and post ranking.

In a post, Facebook made it clear that if you don't scroll past a post and spend some quality time reading it, Facebook considers that post to be valuable to you. To give you more of such posts, the algorithm is designed to go through your contact information and feed you with more similar posts. These are the exact words of Facebook:

> *"Based on the fact that you didn't scroll straight past this post and it was on the screen for more time than other posts that were in your News Feed, we infer that it was something you found interesting and we may start to surface more posts like that higher up in your News Feed in the future."*

Let's assume that this principle is also incorporated into the Instagram algorithm. The implication is simple: the length of time you spend on an Instagram post will be used to determine how many similar posts you will receive in your feed.

While the suggestion that time spent did not emanate from Instagram management, its veracity cannot be ruled out considering that Facebook is Instagram's parent company.

# CHAPTER 10

# USING INSTAGRAM FOR BUILDING A PERSONAL BRAND

You might not know it, but every individual has a brand. You are associated with something. That is exactly what branding means. A personal brand refers to different attributes that are known to a particular individual or organization. Mind you, these attributes can either be positive, negative, or neutral. For example, when you hear of Barack Obama, the first thing that comes to mind is he is a past United States president. Also, if someone mentions Osama bin Laden close to you, you would remember him as a suicide bomber. This is precisely what branding means. It can appear in the form of your name, biography, occupation, skills, behavioral patterns, experience in a particular field, appearance, and some other factors.

As a personal brand, you dictate what people would think of you. Forget your CV or skills; it is your output that would speak highly of you. If you go for a job interview and the interviewer goes through your CV, it doesn't guarantee you a spot in the organization. You shall be required to undergo both oral and written tests. The answers you give are how you will brand yourself. Your CV may not even be perfect, but you can be considered the perfect fit for the job because of the kind of branding you have accorded yourself.

To create a successful personal branding, you need to come up with concrete strategies to make it possible. The perceptions of people about you need to resonate toward three qualities.

Authenticity: There is nothing better than for people to regard you as authentic. This means that you are original and there is nothing substandard about you.

Difference: Do you remember 7 Up's "Dare to be different"? That is precisely what you are. You are quite different, and it has endeared people toward you. You do not conform to the norm.

Best quality: Good is acceptable, better is encouraging, and best is premium. That is exactly what you are–premium. Progressive humans prefer quality over quantity, so you are always their first choice.

**Factors That Affect Personal Brand**

The way you talk: Communication is key in life. Therefore, your talks need to be impeccable, both verbally and nonverbally. You have to accord every human with respect. Consequently, you need to avoid degrading talks.

Education: The form of knowledge you may have received on particular subjects can be a key to determine what many people think of you. If you have sufficient knowledge related to specific topics, you can be highly regarded.

Negotiation skills: It might not look it, but the way you negotiate your way into or out of situations or during a business transaction can affect your branding. If you settle for less, people's perception of you might be affected adversely. However, if you decide to go for more, they can think of you as a quality brand.

Customer service: This is quite important in branding. Individuals and organizations who attend to customers with politeness and ensure their products and services are promptly delivered are highly thought of. If it is otherwise, it can lead to low ratings, and that isn't good for a brand.

Presentation: Brands who present themselves with an aura of confidence are more sought after than those bereft of confidence.

You need to set up a profile for your brand. This profile contains the following information:

"Who we are": You need to explain in lucid terms what you stand for. Your area of specialization, your core business values, your mission and vision statements, and your future projections fall under this category.

"What we do": People need to know what exactly you do. You need to be concise and precise about this.

"What makes us different": Under this category, you need to portray your uniqueness and peculiarity. Highlight what your brand does that is quite uncommon with others. This is an avenue to sell your brand. Use it wisely.

## Instagram Is the Best Media to Grow Your Brand

Instagram isn't only meant for business transactions. As a matter of fact, that is only secondary. It is a medium to connect with people through visuals. You can also build your brand through Instagram. If you are interested in a particular subject and your posts are entirely consistent on this subject, you can be regarded to as a thought leader. That's branding. You should see Instagram as a microblog. People think of Mediatakeout as an entertainment blogging superpower and Forbes as an economic giant. It is the same way you can be associated with a particular niche. As long as you showcase your expertise in a specific subject, your branding can be useful.

If you want to ensure your brand records huge success on Instagram, there are certain things you can do.

Reflect on your brand. You need to be critical of the brand you are building. Be sincere with yourself. Are you satisfied with where you are now? What do you think you can do to improve your brand? These questions can serve as guides for you. Also, you can ask people about their honest opinion of your brand. You should note that the truth might sting, but it is a way to forge ahead and aid your development. You need to be reflective regularly. Also, you can ask for feedback from your followers. Accept their constructive criticism because they are the recipients of your brand. A few people might rubbish you, not because it is true but because of their animosity. Whatever a bulk of them thinks is most likely the truth. It is precisely what you need to work upon.

Define what you desire to be known for. As a brand, you need to be associated with a particular niche or subject. You need to clearly define it so people can correct when you are derailing and place you back on track. Clarity is essential in branding. You need to let people know why you are branding. For a job? It is a great way to sell yourself.

Share frequently. On the path to becoming a thought leader, you can share insights frequently. Focus on contents that will be beneficial to your target audience. You can also mix professionalism and humor. Both can go hand in hand. Ensure they do. However, you need to be careful about what you share too. Sharing a picture with your mentor is cool, but that picture taken while you were downing a few bottles of alcohol should not find their way to Instagram. You need to be civil in all you do. A little mistake can soil your brand.

Meet people in real life. You should stop hiding behind the "introvert" mask. Endeavor to meet some of your followers in real life. Do not limit sharing insights to the internet alone; doing it in person is a great way to build relationships. Also, you can meet to hang out, unwind, and have fun. Forget the Instagram hype, and you are human too. You deserve to act silly too. Also, you can attend productive events. You see those conferences you hear of frequently? They won't participate in themselves. They need people like you to be there and learn a few things that will be beneficial to your brand. Research the conference and find out who is likely to attend. You should also set your mind on the people you would like to meet. It might be an opportunity of a lifetime. Take charge. Also, you can meet people who would present you with massive opportunities. Therefore, you do not have to be confined to your mobile devices. Go out.

Update your profile. We cannot hammer on this one enough. It is an overview of who you are. Make it count. Promote yourself on this profile. You can list your skills and achievements in a concise way. You need the professional image that befits your brand. Acquire it through your profile.

## Strategies That Would Aid Your Brand Growth on Instagram

Every brand wants to grow—at least, that is the goal. How exactly can your brand grow? If you haven't asked yourself this question, you haven't desired growth. You need to put various things into action when developing your brand.

Content strategy: If you need to be reminded, content is king. However, you cannot afford to churn out aimless contents. These contents aid your consistency as a brand. Also, it is the most feasible way of increasing your engagements. This is why you cannot ignore the strategy. You need to use contents shared by established brands with similar niches or subjects as an insight. Compare and contrast both brands. Study what has made them successful.

The contents you want to share need to be goal-oriented, catchy, and witty. You need to stand out from the rest of the pack. Be critical of the type of image you post. It needs to ooze quality. Also, these contents have to be frequent. You need to display contents regularly. People look forward to your contents, so it will be unwise to be irregular with it. They would move on and find another content creator who satisfies their desires.

## Frequent Engagement of Your Audience

Your audience can make or mar your audience. This is why you need to be as close as possible with them. What do they want? This is highly important that needs to be answered. You cannot afford to post contents that are not relatable. You need to understand what they want. Also, do not ignore their comments. It takes a certain level of relationship before Instagram users can post comments. Therefore, reply to them when you can. Do not fail to acknowledge pertinent questions and answer them promptly. Believe it or not, you are like a rabbi who shall be bombarded with questions by students. Provide accurate answers to every question asked. You can check their feeds, too, to acquaint yourself with some of their posts. You can like engaging ones or even repost them. It means a lot to them that a brand they look up to still has ample time to check up on them. You can even make comments on their posts. This will foster your relationships.

## Follow Similar Brands

You need to keep up with similar brands. You might not even get a follow-back from the big brands. Target the relatively smaller brands. You can engage them in relevant conversations. Assert yourself as a brand to reckon with. You can even have productive arguments with them on certain subjects. Giving different opinions of various subjects might even be an eye-opener. You can use your intellectuality as leverage to form a sort of collaboration with them. You can achieve big traction posting each other's contents. You should ensure to give them credits though.

## Post Your Contents Links on Other Platforms

You do realize Instagram is not the only social media platform you use, right? Do not ignore other platforms. They come in handy, especially when you have to promote certain posts on other platforms. All you need to do is simply post a link and add captions. These captions need to portray what they should expect from the posts. It can be an excerpt. The caption needs to be thought-provoking and incomplete. You need to give your audience the desire to click on the content. Chances are if they click on the link and they go through the contents, some of them might even decide to follow you.

## Use Your Call-to-Action Tools Judiciously

You need to pay keen attention to the CTA button. Never use a button that is quite needless for your brand. For example, a haulage company is not expected to the Download button. Only use what resonates with your brand.

## Products and Services Related to Your Brand

This is a subject that needs to be highly dwelt upon. As a brand, you have different products and services that rake in income for you. The social media world is packed with prospective customers and clients who might be interested in your products. However, you need to market products and services that resonate with your brand. It is important that you avoid a conflict of interest. Amassing followers is a way of creating leads. Your followers might be interested in your contents because they are relatable. Therefore, before you advertise a product and service, your contents must act as guides to them. For example, if you own a photography brand, your contents can include how to take the perfect picture, top photo editing apps for mobile devices, most liked pictures on Instagram, sample pictures of clients you have taken before, etc.

## Your Potential Customers

Your products and services determine who your potential customers are. There are different variables that can determine your potential customers.

## Age Grade

The age grade can be a determinant. Unless you sell a general product or service, they cannot be applicable or used by everyone. You need to identify the age group you are targeting.

## Gender

Also, there are products and services peculiar to sexes. Not all products and services can be used by the same sex. Take note of the gender that would be more beneficial to your products and services and focus on them. In essence, if you own a lingerie brand, females should be your target. In the same vein, if you own a Montessori, parents should be your potential customers.

## Region

Since some products and services are region-specific, it is beneficial to focus on people born or who live in such regions. For example, an engineering company that specializes with the assembly and sales of generating sets would rather focus on areas or countries battling with epileptic power supply, e.g., Nigeria, Zimbabwe, Benin Republic, and the likes.

## Interests

Every human has different subjects or events that strike one's interests. Humans share different tastes, and this is notable. Be it music, food, books, movies, or what have you, there are striking differences in what people prefer or like. This is why you need to take cognizance of this.

## Income

You are aware of the fact that not everyone can afford everything. In fact, most humans cannot afford many things. So it is a wise idea for you to put the financial status of people into consideration before choosing your target audience. If you are advertising a luxury product or service, it is advisable for you to focus on wealthy people.

## Why Instagram Ads Is the Best Way to Target Your Audience

If you are looking to reach a target audience with your post, then Instagram ads are your feature of choice. As a paid feature, the onus is on Instagram to identify people who might be interested in your products and services. All you have to do is click on certain keywords and fill out some fields. The app will automatically use its algorithm to derive your target audience for you. This is a reason why Instagram ads are the most effective way to target your audience.

## Reach

As a paid advertisement, the number of people who would have access to your content will more than triple the number of people who view without ads. People who are interested in your brand or niche can be added to your growing community.

## How to Scale Rapidly Your Followers with Instagram Ads

Like it was pointed earlier, Instagram is a community with over 1 billion registered users. This means that there are more than enough people to see your ads. Also, as a brand, it is your desire to increase engagements on your page and your follower count. When you use Instagram ads, your sponsored post is more likely traction. This is also the best way to follow those whose interests resonate with your product and service. You can follow likers and those who make comments. At least 30 percent of them would follower back.

This is one of the reasons why Instagram ads are highly recommended.

# CHAPTER 11

# DEVELOP AN INSTAGRAM MARKETING STRATEGY

You may feel like many others: you know how important it is to be present on Instagram, you want to be active on the platform, but you do not know how to do it the best way. Many companies are forced to advertise their brand on any social network, and they do not take enough time to work out a sophisticated strategy. Since Instagram is quite different from all other social networks, this platform requires a very **individual marketing strategy**. The tips below will help you to find your own personal style for your Instagram appearance.

## Determine your Instagram audience

As with any other platform, you should first determine which audience you want to target. If you already have other marketing strategies, you can use them as a foundation. Then narrow your Instagram audience by setting the following factors: age, location, gender, income, interests, goals, and typical challenges.

but how does it continue? Keep track of popular hashtags on events and topics that are relevant to your business. Find out who's using and interacting with these hashtags and look at the profiles of these Instagram users. You can also look closely at the followers of a competitor. Sometimes it's actually easier than you think to choose your target audience.

## Conduct a competitive analysis

After determining your Instagram audience, you should run a competitive analysis to find out what content your competitors are posting on Instagram. If you already know who your main competitors are, look at their Instagram profiles. If not, you can find similar company profiles by entering search terms that are relevant to your business or industry. Then check what your competitors' contributions get the most attention, which popular hashtags are used, how the captions are designed, how often posts are published, and how successful the companies are. This information will then help you to design and optimize your own Instagram profile.

If you notice in the analysis of the contents of your competitors that they missed a certain chance so far, make a note of them. Because with new content you can stand out from the crowd.

## Set up an editorial calendar

On average, **six photos per week** Posted by companies, that is more than 300 pictures a year. With this amount it is not easy to keep track of which content has already been published and which posts should be posted and when. Here's an editorial calendar to help you significantly reduce the administrative burden of your Instagram account. In this calendar, you can sort your posts by post type (see above), design your captions and hashtags, and create a schedule for posting each post. In addition, the editorial calendar is a great way to capture important events that you want to get noticed on Instagram - such as the launch of a new product or a discount promotion. **Without an editorial calendar** It can happen that you are so busy looking for content ideas that you do not have time to look for current opportunities.

## Pay attention to a uniform brand appearance

If you randomly post content and your posts do not match, you'll confuse your audience and likely lose followers. Therefore, it is important that you find a clear line and pay attention to a uniform brand appearance. It helps to think about your brand personality. What are your brand values? Would you like to present it cheeky, playful, direct or bold?

For example, the lifestyle and interior design experts at **Apartment Therapy** have used the popular concept #foodporn (the appealing presentation of delicious food) in apartments. The brand stands for bright, immaculate, well-structured furnishing concepts and this is exactly what the Instagram presentation of Apartment Therapy reflects. Ideally, a user recognizes at first glance that a photo in their feed comes from you.

Another excellent example of a successful unified presentation of the brand personality is Taco Bell . The company has adapted its feed to the more outspoken style and on-the-go lifestyle of Millennials, its target audience, and focuses on entertaining photo contributions to encourage users to interact.

Once you've defined your brand personality, you can start aligning your content with it. This may even affect the color picker for photos.

Also, focus your posts on the story you want to tell about your brand. Capturing interesting captions in captions helps build a personal relationship between you and your audience. A good example of successful storytelling is **Red Bull's** feed , which contains countless photos and videos of challenging sports situations.

## Convert Instagram followers to customers

Once you have built a solid base of followers, you can take initial action to convert these to paying customers. The following options are available, among others:

- **Promotions:** Promotions, discounts, "Two for the price of one" promotions and similar promotions are great for getting Instagram users up and running for the first time. Make sure you clearly state the terms of the offer and point to the end date of the action to give some urgency.

- **Competitions**: One of the most effective ways to attract new customers is to provide a trial version of your product. As part of the contest , challenge users to follow you on Instagram or tag a post with a specific hashtag.

- **Social engagement:** According to a recent survey , 81% of companies millennials expect public commitment to engage socially. This means that with social engagement, you can increase your brand affinity and your chances of converting followers to customers. An example of this is the fashion label Gap, which supports the organization The Global Fund in the fight against AIDS in Africa. Gap has helped raise more than $ 130 million since 2006.

- **Teaser:** Instagram is perfect for giving your target audience first glimpses of new, upcoming products. But be careful not to flood the feeds of your followers with pure product photos. Post only one or the other photo and thus arouse the curiosity of the users.

- **Live Launch of Products**: In some cases, it's a good idea to give users the ability to track the launch of a product in real time via Instagram Live. You can also encourage viewers to buy directly by inserting a link into their profile to purchase their new product.

# CHAPTER 12

# AFFILIATE MARKETING
# WITH INSTAGRAM

When it comes to making passive income online, Affiliate Marketing, as you probably are aware, is a standout amongst the most utilized wellsprings of income by individual bloggers. On the off chance that you have no clue what partner showcasing is, at that point we will cover what subsidiary advertising is in this section. Additionally, we will talk about precisely how to begin advertising on your blog entry to yield more outcomes.

To clarify how bloggers make cash is truly straightforward. We fabricate trust between the blogger and the reader. When we have figured out how to do as such, we will offer them items which will have a one of a kind connection joined to it. At whatever point your believed group of onlookers chooses to purchase the item suggested by you with the remarkable connection, you make a commission on it.

When you have figured out how to construct a confided in gathering of people, at that point utilizing offshoot promoting to make money would be an extraordinary thought. It is likewise by a wide margin the most easy method for profiting as a blogger since all you need to is compose an incredible article with a HTML connecting to the item. All you should do is discover an item which you like and trust. It ought to likewise give you a subsidiary connection.

Despite the fact that this sounds astonishing, there are numerous interesting points before you can begin acquiring your member bonus. In this section, we will do only that as we will discuss the primary things you have to take care before you can begin profiting from subsidiary showcasing. On the off chance that that sounds great to you, at that point we should begin.

## Marketing 101

Presently to keep things straightforward as a blogger or an author who is simply beginning his or her vocation, all you have to stress over is two offshoot advertising stages. The main two stages are Amazon members and ClickBank. These two offshoot projects will enable you to make the most cash out of your blogging tries.

The distinction between Click-bank and Amazon offshoots is this. ClickBank offers advanced items which are more often than not exactly costly. In spite of the fact that you can make a great deal of benefit or commission out of a Click-bank subsidiary item, you have to ensure that advanced course is identified with your specialty and increases the value of the confided in group of onlookers.

Despite what might be expected, Amazon Affiliates offers a wide scope of items. It could be anything from a book or the most recent and the most astounding tech item in your specialty, so your entrance to boundary it's very huge with Amazon partners. I prescribe you, an apprentice, begin with Amazon Affiliates. Likewise, beginning with a low-value item to try out the waters is an incredible thought.

Thusly you will know whether your group of onlookers acknowledges the item you're endeavoring to offer them. To give you folks a reasonable cautioning, don't hope to profit from low ticket partner showcasing as you will be baffled. Utilize these low-ticket items to try out the waters and to discover what your group of onlookers prefers once you discover scale the items up to a more expensive rate point. Making it simpler for you to win higher commissions, it is in every case better to offer one costly item than it is to sell ten low ticket items over the long haul.

## Stage 1

Your initial step with member promoting is fabricate a confiding in gathering of people. Tragically, you won't make a solitary penny in the event that you don't have an unsuspecting crowd.

First, begin with Amazon offshoots so it would be simpler for you to begin. Initially, compose something like ten blog entries without partner joins, offer individuals free guidance and information on the subject. This will enable you to assemble trust with your gathering of people, when you have composed each one of those ten sites you ought to gradually begin to build up a crowd of people who will have confidence in your insight. Begin by offering them something modest like under $10. On the off chance that you are in the wellness specialty, it could be a book or an enhancement.

## Stage 2

When you have finished Step 1, we will currently get into higher ticket items. This would incorporate ClickBank and Amazon associates, so to quickly address ClickBank. They offer anything you can consider in an online course.

On the off chance that you need to figure out how to cook, ClickBank has a seminar on it. It doesn't make a difference what specialty you're in, you will discover an item to sell. Your objective ought to be to sell a blend of Amazon Affiliates and ClickBank. In the end, this is the place the cash will be.

So once you have discovered what your group of onlookers likes, you can begin offering them computerized items from ClickBank and furthermore begin offering them higher ticket items from Amazon. In case you're into wellness specialty and your gathering of people is progressively disposed towards fat misfortune, you can have an offshoot interface for fat misfortune supplements and a Click-Bank course which will enable them to lose fat.

As should be obvious, subsidiary promoting is exceptionally clear. Following these two stages can enable you to make a decent salary. Yet, recall that you will require a crowd of people to pitch it to which implies having an email list is an absolute necessity.

Center around creating extraordinary substance and following the means you have adapted so far in this book. Something else to observe, don't generally pitch to your gathering of people, regardless of whether you have the most steadfast and confiding in devotees. You ought to give them free substance more regularly than you are selling items. Let's be honest, individuals don't care for it when they tune in to an attempt to sell something. Additionally, remember why these readers joined in any case. It was to become familiar with what you bring to the table them, as opposed to purchasing items or administrations from you.

# CHAPTER 13

# THE HASHTAG LIE

Ah, this is the part that you were probably wondering about. With so many people using hashtags all the time on Instagram, they must be super important. Right?

**Wrong!**

There's actually a hard limit on the amount of hashtags that you should be using. And just because you can post up to 30 hashtags on a picture does not mean that you should. Here is what happens if you go down this route:

Sure, you'll get lots of new followers and an increased amount of likes. You must be getting greater engagement. Not so fast! For one, you are going to attract automation bots that are specifically programmed to like or follow people who post using a certain hashtag. This dilutes your following of engaged followers and decreases your engagement rate over the long-term which annihilates your chances of consistently making it to the Explore page on Instagram. Additionally, you are attracting people that might not see your posts or page, let alone be interested in the niche that you cater to.

In short, using excessive hashtags is just a game of improving your likes and followers for the sake of having higher numbers.

The primary focus of this entire book is to walk you through step-by-step how to generate predictable profits from your Instagram page. And in order to do that successfully you have to create a community of real and engaged followers that genuinely want your content. You cannot develop a loyal follower base by pasting 30 hashtags on each of your Instagram posts.

The maximum number of hashtags you will see on large Instagram

Influencer pages is 5, with 1 to 3 being the norm. Since hashtags lead to engagement from people who don't even see the post, you cannot know when you are receiving true engagement. This is why you should strive to leave any hashtags off of your content when you are testing new and different content strategies.

Leave the game of hashtag oversaturation to people who don't understand the concept of acquiring real and engaged followers. Go the opposite direction and get real engagement that you can utilize to accurately track your growth. With that said, there is no need to completely demonize hashtags. Used sparingly and strategically, they can be yet another useful tool in your arsenal for increasing your follower base and your engagement. Here are some tips for using hashtags on your Instagram page effectively.

## BE SPECIFIC

The most successful Instagram Influencers only use targeted hashtags or ones specific to their brand. You want to model that same approach. Using generic and spam hashtags (anything with a '4' in it) will hurt engagement in the long run because you will be unfollowed for not engaging back through commenting or following them.

Plus, your followers aren't going to your page so that they can be spammed with endless hashtags in each photo. It looks out of place and some of your followers will get the impression that you are a bot-run spam page.

## KEEP HASHTAGS IN THE COMMENTS

This ensures that your picture will be found when a particular hashtag is entered into the search field. It makes your content more accessible to those who are searching for your hashtag but are not following you.

Moreover, your caption is for valuable sales copy that gets people to take action (follow someone, click on the link in the bio, etc.). Don't take up valuable space with distracting hashtags. You can fix this by putting the hashtags in as a comment on the post. Just because this is so important I want to repeat this point and make it crystal clear: DO NOT put hashtags in the caption section of your Instagram post. Put your hashtags in as a comment on your Instagram post.

## ROTATE BETWEEN SETS OF HASHTAGS

Let's say that you have a number of hashtags that have worked well for you, but you know that spamming your content repeatedly with them won't help. Within your niche, you can have a set of hashtags that you sparingly use for specific scenarios. You can have a set of hashtags for posts about your personal life, another set of hashtags for inspirational posts, and perhaps a set of hashtags for your ad shoutouts. This helps you tap into audiences based on search results and you can bring in more engagement to your page.

Ninja Hack: Have your hashtags saved in the notes section of your smartphone so all you have to do is simply copy and paste them into the comments section of your Instagram post.

## DO SOME HASHTAG RESEARCH

Of course, all of the tips above are predicated on doing your due diligence in finding the right hashtags to use. A great tool to use is: SocialRank.com. It's free of charge and allows you to research the key hashtags being used by your successful competitors. You can also find the users that identify most with key terms and the most frequently used hashtags within each of those terms. There are other things you can do with Social Rank, but it really stands out as a great hashtag research tool.

Another great place to learn how to expand on your hashtags is: Hashtagify.me. Visit this website and learn how you can reach a broader audience on Instagram by finding hashtags that are similar to the ones you are currently using.

## GEOTAG YOUR PHOTOS

This is a strategy I have not personally tested, but there are

Instagram Influencers who swear that they have seen increased engagement on their posts from using geotags. Try it for yourself and see if it works for you.

Here, you are geotagging your Instagram photos as a way to add locality to your Instagram posts. I can see where this would be especially useful if you are a local business looking for exposure in your city or town, or operating in a niche involving multiple locations around the world. It turns out that more and more Instagram users are using "Places -> Near Current Location" in the search function. If your post is geotagged and they are searching for something in your niche, you have opened up the door to gain local organic traffic.

In conclusion, hashtags can definitely help you grow your Instagram following as well as act as a navigational tool for helping people find your content. Used correctly and sparingly hashtags will spread your content throughout the Instagram platform. Consider them to be icing on the cake – they are nice to have but your business or brand will not fail because you forgot to use hashtags or you use the incorrect ones. Make sure you have the fundamentals down pat before you start testing out different hashtag strategies.

# CHAPTER 14

# TRICKS TO GET MAXIMUM ENGAGEMENT ON YOUR POSTS

Instagram marketing works, which is why you can expect tons of other brand similar to yours using Instagram to compete for people's attention. And because of that, each year, it gets harder and harder to increase engagement. That doesn't mean, though, that it's impossible to make the most of your posts. In this section, we offer you a few ways you can take your Instagram strategy to another level and get maximum engagement on your Instagram posts.

### Optimize Instagram Story Posts

We've already shared how important it is to prepare your posts well before publishing them online. Instagram uses an algorithm, and you want that algorithm to work on your favor if you are to increase engagement.

There are several ways you can optimize every Instagram story that you publish, and one of them is by using location and hashtag stickers. When Instagram Stories first came out, it only allowed users to share them with their own followers. After several updates, stories you post are now searchable both by hashtag and location. This means anyone can now see your stories.

Another way you can optimize Instagram Stories is by adding links to them. By adding a link, you can lead people wherever you want them to go, such as your blog, to a landing page in your main website, to an affiliate page, or to your email list.

You can also tag other accounts in your Stories to drive more traffic to your content. Alternatively, you can repost user-generated content or UGC if you're working with other business on Instagram. This will go a long way in building relationships and networks in your online community as the account you tag may mention you in return, increasing your profile's visibility.

## Maximize Your Captions

Didn't we already mention what crucial role your captions play in Instagram marketing? And didn't we mention that you can write as many as 2,200 characters in your captions? That would be around 300 to 400 words depending on the type of words you use, and that's more than enough words to share with your audience. Moreover, some of the best brands on Instagram make the most out of their captions, with others even using the comments section if they want to write more about their posts.

Sometimes, one-liners are simply not enough. Talk as much as you can about your brand through your captions to keep your followers informed. Writing a lengthy caption directly on Instagram is easier said than done, however. The caption box isn't just user-friendly enough for you to edit captions quickly and easily. But thank goodness there are now Instagram schedule apps that let you write, review, and edit captions with ease. Some of these apps, such as Later, even let you save your post with your caption and edit it at a later time.

## Make Use of Instagram Stories Stickers

The Instagram Stories feature doesn't only let you share information. More importantly, it lets you converse with your followers, which is crucial if you want them to be constantly engaged and connected to you. One of the easiest ways you can do that is by taking advantage of Instagram Stories stickers.

Instagram Stickers can be incorporated to both image and video stories. Some of these are clickable, some are animated, while others allow your followers to directly interact with your story. Stickers make Instagram posts, particularly stories, more interesting, and this increases the chance of users interacting with your posts. The sticker that you want to use more often are those that let users engage directly with your story, two of which are the Question sticker and the Poll & Vote sticker.

Adding a Question sticker to your post is a great way for followers to get to know your brand better. In the same manner, it's an effective way to find out what your followers want regarding your brand. You can use it to start conversations about what product line your followers want to see next or what design they would recommend for certain products. More importantly, it's an easy way to get customer feedback.

The Poll & Vote sticker works a bit similarly. You can use it to get insights about the preferences of your followers. You can also use it to get your followers to be more aware of your brand. And just as is with the Question sticker, its brevity and simplicity allows you to find out what resonates with your customers with ease.

**Schedule Your Stories**

Instagram Stories are no doubt an excellent form of engagement. But, did you know that you can utilize this feature the incorrect way? And once you do that, you'd be doing more harm to your brand than good. We've talked about in an earlier section the importance of posting at the right day and at the right time, and that principle very much applies to stories.

One way to find out what specific times of the day your followers are active and viewing your Instagram posts the most is through Instagram Insights. It's an analytical tool that provides you with crucial data on the demographics and actions of your followers, as well as the performance of your posts. Within this feature, you will dig a host of information on your profile's performance, including the days and hours your followers are active the most. Knowing when the best time is to post your stories lets you prepare them in advance and schedule them for posting later at the most optimized times.

**Share More About Your Brand**

There's a universal rule in business that states that people will only transact with those whom they can trust. In short, relationship matters. One way you can form and strengthen your brand's relationship with your audience is by being transparent to them. That could mean opening up more about your business. And if there's one place you can do that, it's on Instagram.

Instagram is not only a place where you can post pictures of your products hoping people would buy them. More importantly, it's a place where you can share your passion with the world, let people know why your business exists, and who the people are behind the company. That said, you can increase engagement on your posts by sharing more details about your company, like sharing when you're hiring new staff or ideas you have about future products or improvements on current ones.

## Have a Strong Hashtag Strategy

Hashtags rocketed to fame on Twitter, and now they're found on almost all social media platform. They seem have been taken for granted over the past years, but hashtags are more than just words you use to label your messages. Hashtags are like a compass that point people to your content. Understanding which hashtags to use to drive more people to your posts is the key to increasing your user engagement on Instagram.

Categorizing your hashtags is one way you can make the most out of using them. If you're into food business, for instance, you may be using different hashtags for different topics, ranging from cooking, food preparation, to packaging. Placing each hashtag in a category lets you determine which of the hashtags attract the most engagement.

Instagram analytics helps you find out which of the hashtags you are using are the most effective in drawing people to your posts. There are several ways you can see how many impressions your post has gained, one of which is by clicking "View Insights" at the bottom left corner of a post.

## Spice Up Your Posts

Want to see some real returns in your Instagram posts? If you do, then take time to add some element of fun to your photos, videos, or stories. Of course, you want to stay true to your brand's theme and culture, but that doesn't mean you can't spice up things a little bit. One you can do that is by adding memes from time to time.

## Pay Attention to DMS and Comments

This may be a no-brainer and you're probably good at this already, but so many other brands tend to pay little attention to their DMs. Even comments on feeds are left ignored. The thing about Instagram, just like any other social platform, is that it's founded in communities and relationships. No matter how big you think your brand is, if you don't spend time replying to DMs or comments, time will come when you'll see your following dwindling.

Replying to your follower's comments and messages may be a simple gesture, but it goes a long way in gaining people's trust and strengthening relationships. The more DMs, comments, likes, and shares your posts receives, the more Instagram will recognize them as high-quality content, and the more likely they will be visible to a wider audience.

The goal of paying attention to DMs and comments is not simply for boosting engagement. More importantly, it's to find ways to improve your strategy. More often than not, your followers will leave comments and messages both with positive and negative feedback. Use these feedback, whether positive or negative, as a means to enhance your products and services.

## Partner With an Influencer

Finally, you'd want to collaborate with an influencer if you are to see any increase in user engagement. Influencers are people who have the ability to direct the purchasing decision of others as a result of their authority and knowledge regarding a particular niche. Just because a person is famous and has a large following doesn't necessarily mean that he or she is the right person to partner with. The keyword is "like-minded."

# CHAPTER 15

# HOW TO MAKE MONEY ON INSTAGRAM

One of the neat things about Instagram is that there are a lot of different ways that you can earn money through this platform. While this guidebook has spent a lot of time talking about how businesses can grow their following and earn customers, the same tips can be used for individuals who are looking to earn money online. A business may decide to just sell their own products online to customers and make a profit that way, but there are other methods that small businesses (depending on who they are) and individuals can use to earn a very nice income online from all the hard work they have done to gain followers and a good reputation on this platform. Let's take a look at some of the different ways that you can potentially make money on Instagram.

## Affiliate Marketing

The first option is to work as an affiliate marketer. Basically, with this option, you are going to promote a product for a company and then get paid for each sale. This is something that is really popular with bloggers because they work on getting their website set up, and then they can write articles about a product, or sell advertising space, and then they make money on any sales through their links. You can do the same thing with Instagram as well.

When you want to work with affiliate marketing with Instagram, you need to post attractive images of the products you choose and try to drive sales through the affiliate URL. You will get this affiliate link through the company you choose to advertise with. Just make sure that you are going with an affiliate that offers high-quality products so you don't send your followers substandard products. And check that you will actually earn a decent commission on each one.

Once you get your affiliate URL, add it to the captions of the posts you are promoting or even in the bio if you plan to stick with this affiliate for some time. It is also possible to use the bitly.com extension to help shorten the address or you can customize your affiliate link. It is also possible for you to hook up the Instagram profile and blog so that when people decide to purchase through the link at all, you will get the sale.

If you have a good following on Instagram already, then this method of making money can be pretty easy. You just need to find a product that goes with the theme of your page and then advertise it to your customers. Make sure that the product is high-quality so that your customers are happy with the recommendations that you give.

**Create a Sponsored Post**

Instagram users that have a following that is pretty engaged have the ability to earn some money through the platform simply by creating sponsored content that is original and that various brands can use. To keep it simple, a piece of sponsored product through Instagram could be a video or a picture that is going to highlight a brand or a specific product. These posts are then going to have captions that include links, @mentions, and branded hashtags.

While most brands don't really need a formal brand ambassadorship for the creators of this kind of content, it is pretty common for some of these brands to find certain influencers to help them come up with new content over and over again. However, you must make sure that the brands and the products that you use are a good fit for the image that you worked so hard to create on Instagram. You want to showcase some brands that you personally love and can get behind. Then you can show the followers that you have how this brand is already fitting into your lifestyle so they can implement it as well.

**Sell Pictures**

This one is one that may seem obvious, but it can be a great way for photographers to showcase some of the work that you do. If you are an amateur or professional photographer, you will find that Instagram is the perfect way to advertise and even sell your shots. You can choose to sell your services to big agencies or even to individuals who may need the pictures for their websites or other needs.

If you are posting some of the pictures that you want to sell on your profile, make sure that each of them has a watermark on them. This makes it hard for customers to take the pictures without paying you first. You can also use captions to help list out the details of selling those pictures so there isn't any confusion coming up with it at all.

To make this one work, take the time to keep your presence on Instagram active. This ensures that the right people and the right accounts are following. This is also a good place to put in the right hashtags so that people are able to find your shots. You may even want to take the time to get some engagement and conversations started with big agencies in the photography world who can help you grow even more.

## Promote Your Services, Products, or Business

As we have discussed in this guidebook a bit, if you already run a business, then Instagram can be a good way to market and promote your business. For example, if you already sell some products, use Instagram to post shots of the products, ones that the customer can't already find on your website. Some other ways that you can promote your business through Instagram include:

- Behind the scenes: These are very popular on Instagram. Show your followers what it takes to make the products you sell. Show them some of your employees working. Show something that the follower usually won't be able to see because it is unique and makes them feel like they are part of your inner circle.

- Pictures from your customers: If you pick out a good hashtag and share it with your customers, they will start to use it with some of their own pictures. You can then use this content to help promote your business even more.

- Exclusive offers and infographics: You can take the time to market your services through Instagram with some exclusive offers and infographics of your products. This works really well if the offers are ones the customer wouldn't be able to find anywhere else.

## Sell Advertising Space on Your Page

If you have a large enough following, you may be able to get other brands and companies interested in buying advertising on your profile. They will use this as a way to gain access to your followers in order to increase their own followers, sell a product, or increase their own brand awareness. This is the perfect opportunity for you to make some money from all the hard work that you have done for your own page.

There are many different ways that you can do this. You can offer to let them do a video and then post it as your story, promote a post on your profile, or use any of the other ad options that we discussed above. You can then charge for the type of space they decide to use, the amount of time they want to advertise for, and how big of an audience you are promoting them in front of.

## Become a Brand Ambassador

This is something that is becoming really popular with MLM companies. There is so much competition on Twitter and Facebook that many are turning to use Instagram as a new way to promote their products and get followers that they may not be able to find through other means. And because of the visual aspects of the platform, these ambassadors can really showcase some of the products through pictures and videos.

There are many companies that you can choose from when it comes to being a brand ambassador. Since you have already taken some time to build up your audience and you have a good following, so if you can find a good product to advertise to your followers, you can make a good amount of money. You have to pick out a product that your followers will enjoy, ones that go with the theme of your profile to enhance your potential profits.

As you can see, there are many different options that you can choose from when you want to make some money through your Instagram account. All of the different methods make it perfect no matter what your interests are. After you have some time to build up your own audience and you have quite a few followers already looking at your profile and looking to you for advice, you can leverage this in order to make some money through this social media platform.

# CHAPTER 16

# INSTAGRAM AUTOMATION

After you have mastered the strategies in this book, you can start thinking about automating your Instagram account. This can either add massive value to your business or brand on Instagram or ruin all the hard work that you have done up to this point.

There are dozens of software programs out there that plug into your Instagram account and automate your liking of Instagram user's posts, following and unfollowing Instagram users along with commenting. You program this software to engage with real Instagram accounts and it can dramatically increase your follower base along with drive a ton of traffic to the link in your bio, all on autopilot.

Virtually all the large Instagram Influencers use software like this. However, when you automate your Instagram account, you increase your chances of being banned temporarily or permanently by Instagram. You want to keep your follow and unfollow activity under 800 per day, and no more than 40 follows and/or unfollows per hour. You will want to keep your likes under 1,100 per day, and no more than 60 per hour. Automating commenting can be a bit tricky. Try to only use emojis and do not comment more than 110 times a day, and no more than 15 times an hour.

Always proceed on the side of caution when automating your Instagram account. You should know that the limits I just mentioned apply to Instagram accounts that have been around for awhile (2 months or longer). Violating the amount of actions (likes, comments, follows and unfollows) that Instagram allows its users to engage in per hour is a surefire way to get banned before you get started.

All Instagram accounts are under extra scrutiny when they are first opened. For this reason, you want to limit the use of third party applications that attempt to automate human activities such as the ones I just mentioned. (Automating DMs falls into this category as well) This doesn't mean you can't or shouldn't use automation software on your Instagram account within the first few days you open a new page. It simply means you need to tiptoe into the water.

You want to start off slow when you begin automating your Instagram account (300 likes per day, 500 follows and/or unfollows per day, do not use automated commenting at the beginning) and gradually build up your levels of automation. You would be well-advised to read Instagram's 'Terms of Service' regularly since they are constantly changing how many activities (likes, comments, follows and unfollows) accounts are allowed to engage in per hour. Also, if you are participating in engagement groups (like and comment groups) make sure automating your comments is turned off.

Automation software can be a game-changer. It can dramatically help you grow your follower base by thousands of real Instagram users on autopilot. However, like anything in life where there is a reward, there is always a risk.

I have personally tested virtually every automation software program on the market and there is only one that I have found to safely automate an Instagram users activity. It's called Instajam (GetInstajam.com). And it has helped me safely grow many of my Instagram accounts by 1,700 to 3,300 followers each month like clockwork. This is not an attempt to convince you to use automation software on your Instagram account, but rather to inform you that there is a legitimate way to grow your following without having to manually put in a lot of work.

One of the reasons why I like GetInstajam.com so much is because you are not using the software without professional guidance. The developers of Instajam regulate it and ensure that your activity stays within the regularly updated limits of the Instagram platform. With that being said, it is still your responsibility to know Instagram's Terms of Service before getting started with any automation software.

Here's how Instajam works: Your account will be programmed to engage with real Instagram accounts that will become perfect prospects for the products and services you will be selling on Instagram. Liking, commenting, following – all of that is safely done by the software. You get REAL followers from using this software, and not bots that will saturate your page and decrease the quality of your brand. If Instajam software follows an Instagram user for you and they do not follow you back within 24 hours, the software will automatically unfollow them. Why? Because the main objective is to increase your followers, and currently Instagram only allows you to follow 7,500 Instagram users.

When your Instagram account engages with other Instagram users it induces curiosity in the people who see that you have liked their post, commented on their post and/or followed their Instagram account. If you have set up your Instagram page exactly how I have instructed you to in this book, you will see that hyper-active followers in your niche are going to immediately follow you after Instajam engages with their Instagram account. Why? Because of something called the law of reciprocity.

> *"The law of reciprocity, (which applies in EVERY culture on the face of the earth), simply explains that when someone gives you something you feel an obligation to give back. Giving and receiving favors is a common exchange and is an implicit assumption in most relationships."*

The way the law of reciprocity works on Instagram is when you engage with an Instagram users account, they feel compelled to engage with yours. Why? Because when you do something nice for them such as like their post, comment on their post or follow them, they will want to do something nice for you. This typically results in them following your Instagram page and engaging with your posts.

The best part about this software is that you don't need to be online when it is automating your liking, following, unfollowing and commenting. GetInstajam.com is cloud-based software that will continue to grow your account while you are away from your phone. You could be in a meeting, sleeping, or playing with your children and Instajam will be hard at work growing your Instagram following for you.

Remember this: If you are using this software and you are not seeing lots of people follow you back (1,000 or more per month), it's likely the case that your Instagram profile and the content you are creating needs work.

You can check out this amazing software and see if it works as well for you as it has for me.

Disclaimer: I do have a vested interest in www.GetInstajam.com. I helped with the development of this software because I saw so many Instagram users using similar Instagram automation software and they were getting their accounts banned left and right.

What makes GetInstajam.com unique is that to date they have never had an account banned due to breaking Instagram's Terms of Service. Something else that makes this software unique is the extraordinary amount of research that goes into targeting the perfect prospects that your Instagram account will be programmed to engage with. Instajam's automation software is constantly refining who your Instagram account interacts with. This constant refinement allows you to hone in and target people who will love your content and who will eventually become your customers or clients.

Many other similar software out there do not do any research at all and simply just program your account to engage with people who could careless about your content and will never buy your products and services. Other software programs on the market allow you to dangerously automate your Instagram account yourself.

If you're an expert in automation and have a deep understanding of where your perfect prospect is on Instagram and what their dreams and desires are, automating your Instagram account by yourself may work for you. But my experience suggests that most people will substantially increase their following and their bank account balances if they will leave programming their Instagram accounts to the professionals.

# CONCLUSION

Anything is possible with regards to profiting on the web, particularly with a great many people depending on the web to get their data. I trust you delighted in this book, and I want to be similarly as great and help to you. Presently go on and profit you have needed to.

Start making money today and expand your business with Instagram.

Printed in Poland
by Amazon Fulfillment
Poland Sp. z o.o., Wrocław

53421783R00058